SIMPLY THE BEST
UNIVERSAL MIXER RECIPES

MARIAN GETZ

INTRODUCTION BY WOLFGANG PUCK

AS I LEARNED LONG AGO, ALONGSIDE MY MOTHER AND GRANDMOTHER, YOU SHOULD ALWAYS PUT LOTS OF LOVE INTO EVERYTHING YOU COOK. THIS IS CERTAINLY EVIDENT IN THIS COOKBOOK.

Wolfgang Puck

Your universal mixer will change the way you bake forever. The ability to mix to correct consistency depends largely on your ability to add ingredients correctly and monitor them without having an obstructed view from the mixer's head of traditional mixers. No longer do you have to stop the mixing process to scrape down the sides of the bowl thanks to the scraper attachment which allows for a much more efficient mixing task, especially given the powerful motor of this great appliance.

Marian was thrilled to write a cookbook to accompany this mixer. She instantly thought of dozens of recipes to include in this cookbook. Her experience as a pastry chef, wife, mother, and grandmother allowed Marian to put together a cookbook with a wide variety of recipes that I'm sure you will use for years to come.

A student of cooking is probably one of the best ways to describe Marian. She is always looking for something new, something fresh, something local, something seasonal. Her culinary knowledge combined with her passion for cooking is second to none. The recipes that Marian has written for this cookbook will motivate you to be more creative in the kitchen.

INTRODUCTION BY WOLFGANG PUCK

2 Introduction By Wolfgang Puck
6 Helpful Tips
9 Pantry Tips

109 Source Page
110 Index

TABLE OF CONTENTS

RECIPES

10 Mixing Bowl Rose Cake
12 Mashed Potatoes
13 Easy Baked Alaska
14 Cheese Ball
16 Chocolate Meringue Pie
17 Limoncello & Raspberry Semifreddo
18 Really Easy Buttercream
19 Chocolate Rainbow Cake
20 Bacon Wrapped Meatloaf
21 Wolfgang's Kugelhopf
22 Halloween Cheese Ball
24 Iced Sugar Cookies
26 Animal Cupcakes
27 Pumpkin Mousse Parfait
28 Bullseye Cheesecake
30 Strawberry Dessert "Lasagna"
31 Peanut Butter & Jelly Cookies
32 Cheddar Bacon Jalapeño Bread
34 Oatmeal Chocolate Chip Cookies
35 Multigrain Bread
36 Easy Fruit Cobbler
37 Lemon Pound Cake
38 Cheese Soufflé
40 Basic White Bread
41 Date Oat Energy Bites
42 Lava Cake
44 Jalapeño Cornbread
45 Buffalo Chicken Mini Boats
46 Pecan Mashed Sweet Potatoes
47 Spinach Artichoke Dip
48 Oliver's Gluten-Free Brioche
49 Wolfgang's Favorite Cookies

50 No Churn Cherry Ice Cream
52 Old Fashioned Blueberry Coffee Cake
53 Crinkle Cookies
54 Melted Snowman Cupcakes
56 Chocolate Cactus Cupcakes
57 Mocha Fudge Brownies
58 Broiled Oatmeal Cake
60 Grandma's Meatballs
61 BBQ Chicken Cheesy Bread
62 Carrot Raisin Bread
63 Mashed Potato "Frosted" Meatloaf
64 Tomato Focaccia
65 Pizza Dough
66 Dulce de Leche Pie
67 Cinnamon Rolls
68 Old Fashioned Animal Crackers
70 Old Fashioned Whipped Cream
71 Homemade Pie Crust
72 Limeade Freezer Pie
73 Triple Layered Chocolate Towers
74 Easy Hazelnut Cookies
75 Apple Cake
76 Million Dollar Dip
77 Smoked Salmon Dip Roll-Ups
78 Savory Blue Cheese Cheesecake
79 Sweet Potato Dinner Rolls
80 Watercolor Jelly Roll Cake
82 Crème Cake with Grapefruit Glaze
83 Chocolate Mousse
84 Swiss Meringue
85 Cream Puffs
86 French Macaron Cookies

88 Real French Onion Dip

89 Whipped Corn & Ricotta Dip

90 Bacon Horseradish Dip

91 Cheddar Biscuits

92 Best Shepherd's Pie

93 Kitchen Sink Cookies

94 Sprinkle Marshmallows

96 Vanilla Tall Cake

98 Cheeseburger Pinwheels

99 Pimento Cheese Dip

100 Seeded Raisin Bread

101 Cheesy Pretzel Bites

102 Cherry Upside Down Cake

104 Banana Cream Pie

105 Piña Colada Fruit Dip

106 No Bake Raspberry Swirl Cheesecake

107 Crispy Sweet Corn Fritters

108 Zucchini Muffins

TABLE OF CONTENTS

HELPFUL TIPS

Below please find some tips that will help you make the most out of your new mixer.

Mixer Attachments

Choosing the right attachment is important to achieve the best mixing result. Use the whisks for foods that are thin in consistency or need to have a lot of air whipped into them. Most of the time you will be using the scraper attachment along with the paddles or whisks. Exceptions are items like meringues or egg whites that will billow above the scraper attachment if mixed with the scraper in place. The recipes will specify when not to use the scraper. Batters that are of medium consistency are generally made using the paddles. Heavy or stiff doughs are best mixed using the dough hook with pusher attachment. Each recipe in this book will state which attachments to use. For beating egg whites, it is important to make sure all attachments coming into contact with the egg whites are completely clean and free of any fat in order to achieve full volume. For whipped cream, you will achieve better volume if you first chill the mixer bowl and the whisks.

Lid

The lid for the mixer bowl is comprised of two parts, the outer bowl lid and center lid. In general, it is best to use both parts of the lid to prevent any of the ingredients from splashing out during mixing. In cases where you add additional ingredients during the mixing process, you can use the outer bowl lid without the center lid which leaves an opening for you to add ingredients. For very splashy recipes such as whipped cream before it thickens, always use both parts of the lid to prevent a mess in your kitchen.

Mixer Speed Settings

You mixer has 5 speed settings from low to high. In general, use lower speeds when adding additional ingredients or when mixing heavy ingredients such as bread doughs. High speed is generally used to incorporate lots of air into a recipe such as whipped cream or meringue. Adding ingredients on lower speeds helps keep them in the bowl and prevents making a mess all over your counter.

Mixing Time

You will notice that several recipes will suggest a mixing time followed by "mixing time might be shorter". This is because all of cooking is not an exact science. In addition to time, there's typically another indicator stated as to when a mixing step is completed such as "until stiff peaks form" so your actual mixing time may vary. If a recipe states "until time is complete" then you can just let the mixer run for the set time as the mixed ingredients will naturally be mixed with the desired outcome when time is up.

Baking Tips

Baking is often thought of as a difficult task requiring a lot of knowledge and skill. The truth is that anyone can bake if you know these five main things to ensure baking success every time:

- Measure accurately every time.

- Use good equipment, even if it is basic.

- Know your oven well, if its temperature is accurately calibrated and use an oven thermometer.

- Use nonstick baking spray, the kind made with flour, not butter or regular nonstick spray. It is specifically made so that it ensures that your cake will release from the pan in pristine shape. Use it generously, covering all parts of the interior of the pan right before you are going to pour the batter into it.

- Use a timer, the kind that can travel with you from room to room such as your phone or smart watch.

Be Organized

Be organized and read through the recipe once completely. Gather all the ingredients together before you start to measure or mix anything.

Accurate Measuring

Accurate measuring is critical to achieving success in baking. Use glass measuring cups with measurement markings for liquid ingredients and metal measuring cups for dry ingredients. The measuring spoons I prefer are long and narrow so they will fit in the neck of a spice jar.

Measuring in Piles

I recommend measuring in piles to keep track of ingredients. For example, in the mixer bowl, add the flour, then a separate pile of sugar, a separate pile of baking powder etc. Drop those ingredients into separate little piles but close together then repeat with the rest of the ingredients. This allows you to review the ingredients you have already used and keep track of what needs to be added. If you mix all the ingredients together, you will be more likely to forget ingredients which will result in an undesired outcome and may discourage you from baking in the future.

Prevent Sticking

To prevent baked goods from sticking, use parchment paper, nonstick baking spray, or nonstick aluminum foil (which is coated with silicone for easy release).

Baking

Use nonstick baking spray generously then fill your baking vessel such as a baking pan, metal mixing bowl or cupcake mold no more than 2/3 full of batter to leave enough room for it to rise in the oven. Bake cakes in the center of the oven, rotating them halfway through the baking cycle, and place an empty rack above the cake if possible. You can place an empty sheet pan on the empty rack if your cake darkens too fast as it will deflect much of the heat and reduce overbrowning.

Baking Temperature & Time Guidelines

The baking temperature and baking times listed in the recipes are suggestions rather than exact numbers. Many factors influence the baking times such as the quality of the ingredients and the calibration and quality of your oven. In addition, the size of the pan used also affects how long something needs to be baked. For example, a cupcake bakes in far less time than a large cake. One of the most frequently asked questions in the culinary world is how to tell when food is done? The best way to test most baked goods such as cakes and cupcakes for doneness is to insert a wooden pick or bamboo skewer off-center. When removed, it should generally come out with just a few moist crumbs clinging to it. A streak of shiny batter on the wooden pick indicates that additional baking time is needed. You can also test doneness using a thermometer. Your cakes and cupcakes are done when the internal temperature measured at the center registers 200°F on the thermometer. For brownies and cookies, the top should be dry and a knife inserted in the center should come out clean. Cheesecakes are done when they jiggle but not ripple or when the internal temperature at the center measures 155°F using a thermometer.

Leveling Cakes

If your cake emerges from the oven with a peak or hump in the middle, wait until cool then use a serrated knife to cut off all parts of the hump until cake is level. A leveled cake makes for a more professional looking cake, especially once frosted. Do not split cake layers as it creates a large amount of loose crumbs and makes the layers less stable. When you don't split layers, you won't need a crumb coat of frosting in addition to a final coat, making it much faster to frost the cake in one step.

Let Cool

Your baked goods such as cakes or cupcakes need to be completely cool before decorating. Never try to frost a cake that is still warm or the buttercream will melt.

Salt

The salt used in this book is Diamond Crystal Kosher Salt. It is half as salty as most other brands. This is because the grains are very fluffy and therefore not as many fit into a measuring spoon. This brand also lists only "salt" as the ingredient which is great. Most other brand have ingredients that are not natural and ruin the taste. If you are using salt other than Diamond Crystal Kosher Salt, simply use approximately half the amount specified in the recipe. Smoked salts, available in many grocery stores and online, are a great way to add flavor to steamed foods as well.

Butter

All butter used in this book is unsalted. Cool butter is butter that has been left at room temperature for about 30 minutes until cool and waxy when pressed with your thumb. It should not be rock hard, shiny or soft to the touch. Slicing cool butter very thin (about 1/8-inch thin) is best for adding to the mixer while making buttercream. Softened butter means butter that has been left at room temperature for several hours. It should be soft enough to offer no resistance whatsoever when sliced using a knife. While there is no perfect substitute for the pure flavor of butter, you can use a substitute such as vegan butter, coconut oil or margarine and most of the recipes will turn out fairly well.

Vanilla

I adore vanilla and order both my vanilla extract and vanilla beans from a supplier directly from the island of Tahiti. I use both of these in recipes where the vanilla flavor takes center stage. In recipes where vanilla is not the star flavor, I use imitation vanilla because it is less expensive and adds the right amount of taste and aroma without overpowering the other flavors.

Sugar Substitute

While substitutes do not bake as perfectly as regular sugar, they are ok to use if you prefer them. Sugar-free cake mixes will turn out fine.

Chocolate

Buy good quality chocolate and cocoa whenever possible. It is easy to find excellent chocolate at most grocery stores but it is almost impossible to find good quality cocoa powder. Please see the source page 109 for places online to buy good quality cocoa powder.

PANTRY TIPS

Being prepared to cook or bake the recipes in this book, or any recipe for that matter, is one of the keys to success in the kitchen. Your pantry must be stocked with the basics. We all know how frustrating it can be when you go to the cupboard and what you need is not there. This list includes some of the ingredients you will find in this book and some that I feel are important to always have on hand.

PERISHABLES	REFRIGERATED	FREEZER
Apples	Butter	Raspberries
Lemons	Eggs	Blueberries
Limes	Sour Cream	Ice Cream
Grapefruit	Cream Cheese	Mixed Vegetables
Potatoes	Heavy Cream	Corn Kernels
Sweet Potatoes	Whole Milk	
Onions	Full-Fat Buttermilk	
Carrots	Cheeses	
Celery		
Jalapeño Peppers		
Green Onions		
DRY GOODS		
Flour or Gluten-Free Flour	Boxed Pudding Mixes	Olive oil
Cornstarch	Unflavored Gelatin	Honey
Baking Powder	Powdered Sugar	Corn Syrup
Baking Soda	Vanilla	Sweetened Condensed Milk
Salt	Clear Imitation Vanilla	Crackers and Dippers
Sugar & Brown Sugar	Coconut Flakes	Mayonnaise
Yeast	Good Quality Cocoa	Spices
Apple Cider Vinegar	Good Quality Chocolates	Nuts
Maraschino Cherries	Gel or Paste Food Colorings	Matcha Powder (Green Tea)
Raisins	Sprinkles	Molasses
Peanut Butter	Limoncello Liqueur	Dates
Jams & Jellies	Shortening	Oats
Canned Pumpkin Puree	Vegetable Oil	

It is not necessary to have all the items listed at all times. However, if you are feeling creative, adventurous or just following a recipe, it's great to have a good selection in the kitchen.

MIXING BOWL
ROSE CAKE

Makes 1 cake

Ingredients:

1 3/4 cups granulated sugar

1/2 cup unsalted butter, softened

1/2 cup solid white shortening

1 teaspoon kosher salt

1 tablespoon baking powder

1 teaspoon vanilla extract

1/4 teaspoon butter extract

1/8 teaspoon almond extract

5 large egg whites

2 3/4 cups cake flour

1 cup whole milk

Really Easy Buttercream (see recipe on page 18)

Food coloring as desired

Method:

1. *Preheat oven to 350°F and apply nonstick baking spray to a 2-quart stainless steel mixing bowl; set aside.*
2. *Fit mixer with paddles and scraper then add sugar, butter, shortening, salt and baking powder.*
3. *Add outer lid then set timer to 8 minutes (mixing time might be shorter).*
4. *Mix on speed 3 for 5 minutes then pause, add extracts and egg whites then continue mixing until smooth.*
5. *Pause again, add remaining ingredients, except buttercream and food coloring, then mix on speed 2 until just blended.*
6. *Spoon batter into prepared bowl.*
7. *Bake in lower third of oven for 60-70 minutes or until browned and a wooden pick inserted off-center comes out with just a few moist crumbs clinging to it.*
8. *If top of cake darkens too much after 30 minutes of baking, cover loosely with aluminum foil.*
9. *Remove and let cool for 10 minutes before removing from bowl.*
10. *Divide buttercream into three small bowls then color into light, medium and dark pink.*
11. *Fit piping bag(s) with rose tip(s) then pipe circles from top to bottom. Use dark buttercream for the top third, medium for the middle third and light for the bottom third of the cake.*
12. *Serve as desired.*

MASHED POTATOES

Makes 6 servings

Ingredients:

5 pounds Russet or Yukon gold potatoes, peeled and quartered

Kosher salt to taste

4 tablespoons unsalted butter + more for serving

1 1/2 cups or more half & half, cream or whole milk

Fresh pepper to taste

Method:

1. *Place potatoes and salt into a stockpot and cover by 1-inch cold water.*
2. *Bring to a boil over high heat then lower to a gentle simmer.*
3. *Boil for 20 minutes or until fork tender.*
4. *Drain thoroughly then return to heat for 1 minute to dry excess water.*
5. *Fit mixer with whisks (no scraper) then add potatoes and butter.*
6. *Add outer lid and set timer to 2 minutes.*
7. *Mix on speed 4 just until chunks are broken up.*
8. *Add enough dairy to make potatoes soft and smooth (don't over mix).*
9. *Salt and pepper to taste, top with additional butter then serve hot.*

EASY BAKED ALASKA

Makes 6 servings

Ingredients:

1 store-bought pound cake, sliced

1 quart ice cream or sorbet, softened

6 large egg whites

1/4 teaspoon cream of tartar

2/3 cup granulated sugar

Method:

1. *Cover the bottom of a heat-proof serving platter with pound cake slices.*
2. *Place ice cream on top of pound cake, smooth using a spatula then place in the freezer.*
3. *If you do not have a blowtorch, preheat the broiler to high.*
4. *Fit clean mixer with clean whisks (no scraper) then add the egg whites.*
5. *Add outer lid then set timer to 7 minutes (mixing time might be shorter).*
6. *Mix on speed 3 for 20 seconds or until foamy then add the cream of tartar.*
7. *Mix for an additional 20 seconds then begin adding the sugar slowly while continuing to mix for 3-4 minutes or until stiff peaks form (test peaks by stopping mixer and inserting a spoon into the meringue).*
8. *Pile meringue over ice cream until completely covered including the pound cake.*
9. *Brown meringue using a blowtorch or broil for 1-2 minutes until brown.*
10. *Serve immediately.*

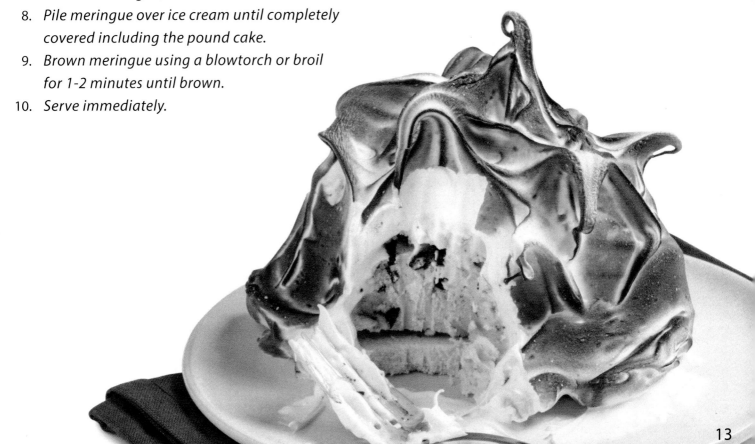

CHEESE BALL

Makes 8-10 servings

Ingredients:

For the Cheese Ball

3 packages (8 ounces each) cream cheese, softened

2 cups Cheddar cheese, shredded

1 tablespoon Worcestershire sauce

Kosher salt and fresh pepper to taste

4 garlic cloves, chopped

1 bunch green onions, chopped

Hot sauce to taste

Zest and juice from 1 lemon

For Decorating

1 bunch fresh parsley, chopped

2 cups grape tomatoes, halved

1/2 cup almonds, sliced

1/2 cup black olives, sliced

1 yellow bell pepper, cut into star shape

Assorted crackers

Method:

1. *Fit mixer with paddles and scraper then add all cheese ball ingredients.*
2. *Add lid then set timer to 5 minutes.*
3. *Mix on speed 3 until time is complete.*
4. *Using oiled hands or wearing gloves, form cheese ball into a cone shape.*
5. *Wrap cone in plastic wrap then refrigerate for several hours until firm.*
6. *Roll entire cone in parsley until evenly covered then place on a serving tray.*
7. *Press in alternating spirals of tomatoes, almonds and olives.*
8. *Top with bell pepper star using a wooden pick to secure.*
9. *Serve with crackers.*

TIP

You can get creative and use other foods to decorate this tree. Tiny crackers arranged in a row can look like "lights" and pickled jalapeño pepper rings can look like "ornaments".

CHOCOLATE MERINGUE PIE

Makes one 8-inch pie

Ingredients:

3 ounces unsweetened chocolate, melted

1 cup unsalted butter, softened

1 cup granulated sugar

2 teaspoons vanilla extract

4 large pasteurized eggs

Homemade Pie Crust, baked (see recipe on page 71)

Swiss Meringue (see recipe on page 84)

Method:

1. *Fit mixer with whisks and scraper then add chocolate, butter and sugar.*
2. *Add lid then set timer to 8 minutes.*
3. *Mix on speed 5 for 4 minutes.*
4. *Pause mixer, add vanilla and eggs then mix for remaining 4 minutes.*
5. *Pour mixture into pie crust then refrigerate for 2 hours.*
6. *Pipe meringue on top as desired then brown using a blowtorch.*
7. *Serve immediately.*

LIMONCELLO & RASPBERRY
SEMIFREDDO

Makes 8 servings

Ingredients:

2 cups fresh or frozen raspberries + more for topping

1/2 cup granulated sugar

1/2 cup limoncello liqueur

3 cups heavy cream, very cold

1 cup powdered sugar

Method:

1. Refrigerate mixer bowl and whisks for 10 minutes.
2. Apply nonstick baking spray to a loaf pan then line with parchment paper and spray again; set aside.
3. In a medium bowl, combine raspberries, sugar and limoncello; let stand for 10 minutes.
4. Fit mixer with chilled bowl, whisks and scraper then add cream and powdered sugar.
5. Add both pieces of the lid then set timer to 5 minutes (mixing time might be shorter).
6. Mix on speed 5 just until soft peaks form.
7. Place a layer of cream mixture into loaf pan then drizzle with some raspberry mixture.
8. Repeat layers until all the cream is used then reserve any unused raspberry mixture.
9. Place in freezer for 2-3 hours or until firm but not hard.
10. Unmold onto a serving plate, drizzle with reserved raspberry mixture then top with additional raspberries before serving.

REALLY EASY BUTTERCREAM

Makes 4 cups

Ingredients:

3 sticks (1 1/2 cups) unsalted butter, cut into very thin slices, cool but not hard

1 cup shortening

1/2 teaspoon clear imitation vanilla extract

1 can (14 ounces) sweetened condensed milk

A pinch of kosher salt

Food coloring as desired

Method:

1. *Fit mixer with whisks and scraper then add butter and shortening.*
2. *Add outer lid then set timer to 15 minutes (mixing time might be shorter).*
3. *Mix on speed 5 for 5 minutes or until smooth and fluffy.*
4. *Add remaining ingredients, except food coloring, then continue to mix on speed 5 until mixture is light, fluffy and smooth.*
5. *To color buttercream, separate the amount of buttercream you want to color into separate bowls then stir in food coloring using a spoon until desired color is achieved.*

TIP

To make strawberry buttercream for the French Macaron Cookies on page 86, place 2 bags (1-ounce each) freeze-dried strawberries into a food processor until powdered. Stir powder into finished buttercream. Freeze-dried fruit is usually sold in the healthy snack area of most grocery stores.

CHOCOLATE RAINBOW CAKE

Makes 1 cake

Ingredients:

1 teaspoon kosher salt

1 teaspoon baking powder

2 teaspoons baking soda

3/4 cup cocoa powder

2 cups granulated sugar

1 3/4 cups all purpose flour

1 cup buttermilk

1/2 cup vegetable oil

2 large eggs

2 teaspoons vanilla extract

1 cup cold coffee

Really Easy Buttercream (see recipe on page 18)

Food coloring as desired

Method:

1. Preheat oven to 350°F and apply nonstick baking spray to two 8-inch cake pans; set aside.
2. Fit mixer with whisks and scraper then add all ingredients in the order listed, except buttercream and food coloring.
3. Add lid then set timer to 4 minutes.
4. Mix on speed 2 for 1 minute then increase to speed 4 and mix until time is complete.
5. Divide batter between prepared pans.
6. Bake in center of oven for 25-30 minutes or until risen and a wooden pick inserted off-center comes out with just a few moist crumbs clinging to it.
7. Remove and let cool for 10 minutes before removing from pans then let cool completely.
8. Divide buttercream between six small bowls then color each with a different rainbow color.
9. Fill and stack cake then use a piping bag (without a tip) for each color.
10. Pipe thick bands of different colors starting from bottom to the top of the cake. Don't worry if it looks a little messy or if some cake shows through.
11. Use a side scraper and a steady hand to smooth and blend frosting as well as remove any excess.

BACON WRAPPED MEATLOAF

Makes 4-6 servings

Ingredients:

1 pound ground beef

1 large egg

2 tablespoons soy sauce

3 white bread slices, torn into bits

1/3 cup whole milk

1 small yellow onion, chopped

1 teaspoon dried sage

2 teaspoons kosher salt or to taste

1/2 teaspoon freshly ground pepper

8 bacon slices

Method:

1. *Preheat oven to 350°F and apply nonstick cooking spray to a loaf pan; set aside.*
2. *Fit mixer with dough hook and pusher attachment then add all ingredients, except bacon.*
3. *Add lid then set timer to 2 minutes.*
4. *Mix on speed 1 until time is complete, scraping bowl as necessary.*
5. *Lay bacon slices in loaf pan with slices slightly overlapping and ends hanging over sides.*
6. *Scoop meat mixture on top of the bacon slices in pan.*
7. *Bring each slice of bacon up and over top of loaf to seal then place pan on a sheet pan.*
8. *Bake for 1 hour or until internal temperature registers 165°F on a meat thermometer.*
9. *When baking is complete, remove, garnish as desired and serve.*

WOLFGANG'S KUGELHOPF

Makes 1 large cake

Ingredients:

1 2/3 cups whole milk

2 tablespoons rapid rise yeast

1/2 cup powdered milk

1/3 cup honey

2 teaspoons vanilla extract

1 tablespoon Stroh rum (optional)

1 teaspoon apple cider vinegar

Zest of 1 orange

3 large egg yolks

2 large eggs

5 cups bread flour

1/2 cup unsalted butter, softened

1 cup dark raisins

1 cup dried apricots, diced

1 cup whole almonds

Method:

1. *Generously apply nonstick baking spray to a 12-inch tube pan.*
2. *Fit mixer with dough hook and pusher attachment then add all ingredients, except butter, raisins, apricots and almonds.*
3. *Add lid then set timer to 15 minutes.*
4. *Mix on speed 1 for 10 minutes then add butter and mix for 2 minutes.*
5. *Add raisins, apricots and almonds and mix until evenly distributed.*
6. *Remove dough hook attachment then cover and let rise for 40 minutes.*
7. *Scrape dough into tube pan, cover and let rise a second time for 40 minutes.*
8. *Preheat oven to 350°F and bake for 40 minutes.*
9. *Cover loosely with aluminum foil then bake for an additional 40 minutes or until well browned and internal temperature registers 200°F on a thermometer.*
10. *Remove and let cool before serving.*

TIP

If you do not have a tube pan you can use a 6-quart stainless steel bowl instead. Generously apply nonstick baking spray to the bowl then fashion the tube part by wrapping a paper cup in aluminum foil and spraying it with nonstick baking spray. To hold the paper cup down as the dough rises, add a handful of stainless steel forks and knives to the cup.

21

HALLOWEEN CHEESE BALL

Makes 8-10 servings

Ingredients:

3 packages (8 ounces each) cream cheese, softened

2 cups Cheddar cheese, shredded

5 bacon slices, cooked and crumbled

Kosher salt and fresh pepper to taste

Bottled hot sauce to taste

1 red bell pepper, diced small (save stem)

1 package (1 ounce) dry ranch dressing mix

1 bunch green onions, chopped

2 cups cheese crackers, crushed

A few kale leaves, for decorating

1 can whole black olives, pitted

Crackers, for serving

TIP
For a vegetarian option, you can make this recipe using the Pimento Cheese Dip on page 99.

Method:

1. Fit mixer with paddles and scraper then add all ingredients except crushed cheese crackers, kale, olives and crackers for serving.
2. Add lid then set timer to 5 minutes.
3. Mix on speed 3 until time is complete.
4. Using oiled hands, shape mixture into a ball then wrap in plastic wrap.
5. Refrigerate for several hours or up to 3 days until firm.
6. Roll ball in crushed crackers to coat then transfer ball onto a serving tray.
7. Loosely lay a clean sheet of plastic wrap over the ball then use a butter knife and your fingers to shape into a pumpkin.
8. Remove plastic wrap then add reserved bell pepper stem and tuck a few kale leaves around the pumpkin.
9. Cut some of the olives into 8 wedges each for the spider legs.
10. Cut several olives in half for the spider bodies.
11. Press bodies and 8 legs each randomly over cheese ball then serve with crackers.

ICED SUGAR COOKIES

Makes 3 dozen cookies

Ingredients:

For the Cookies

1 1/2 cups unsalted butter

2 cups granulated sugar

1 teaspoon butter extract

1 teaspoon vanilla extract

4 large eggs

1 teaspoon kosher salt

1/4 teaspoon baking powder

5 cups all purpose flour

For the Icing

4 cups powdered sugar

4 tablespoons meringue powder

6 tablespoons warm water

Food coloring as desired

Method:

1. Line two sheet pans with parchment paper then set aside.
2. Fit mixer with paddles and scraper then add butter, sugar and both extracts.
3. Add outer lid then set timer to 6 minutes (mixing time might be shorter).
4. Mix on speed 3 for 3 minutes then add the eggs and mix until uniform.
5. Reduce to speed 1 then add salt, baking powder and flour.
6. Mix just until incorporated then refrigerate for 2 hours.
7. Roll out dough between two sheets of plastic wrap then cut out cookies.
8. Use plastic wrap to aid in lifting cookies onto the sheet pans so that they don't distort.
9. Bake for 10-12 minutes or until set but still pale in color.
10. Remove and let cool completely.
11. While cookies are baking, make the icing by whisking together all icing ingredients, except food coloring, in a small bowl until smooth. Color as desired.
12. Outline each cookie with icing using a small piping bag or squeeze bottle.
13. Let dry for a few minutes then decorate cookies with icing as desired.
14. Let icing dry until hard before serving.

ANIMAL
CUPCAKES

Makes 12 cupcakes

Ingredients:

1 cup unsalted butter, softened	1 cup whole milk
2 1/3 cups granulated sugar	1 cup sour cream
5 large eggs	1 tablespoon vanilla extract
3 cups cake flour	1/4 cup rainbow sprinkles + more for topping
3/4 teaspoon baking soda	1 can (16 ounces) fudge frosting
2 1/4 teaspoons baking powder	Store-bought fondant
1 teaspoon kosher salt	Food coloring as desired

Method:

1. *Preheat oven to 350°F and line cupcake tins with papers; set aside.*
2. *Fit mixer with whisks and scraper then add the butter and sugar.*
3. *Add lid then set timer to 4 minutes.*
4. *Mix on speed 3 for 1 minute.*
5. *Add eggs and mix on speed 3 for 1 minute.*
6. *Reduce to speed 1 then add flour, baking soda, baking powder and salt; mix for 30 seconds.*
7. *Add remaining ingredients, except frosting, fondant and food coloring then mix on speed 1 for 30 seconds.*
8. *Fill cupcake wells 3/4 full of batter.*
9. *Bake for 20-22 minutes or until a wooden pick inserted in the center comes out clean.*
10. *Remove and let cool completely then top with fudge frosting and additional sprinkles.*
11. *To make the animals, use small colored fondant balls for each body part then use your fingers and a wooden pick to shape them as desired then assemble using a bit of water as "glue".*

TIP
These cupcakes are also delicious without the fondant animals if you are pressed for time.

26

PUMPKIN MOUSSE PARFAIT

Makes 8 servings

Ingredients:

3 cups heavy cream, very cold

1 can (15 ounces) pumpkin puree

1 1/4 cups light brown sugar, packed

2 tablespoons ground pumpkin spice

A pinch of kosher salt

1 tablespoon vanilla extract

1 teaspoon butter extract

1 cup gingersnap cookie crumbs

Candy corn and gingerbread cookies, for garnishing

Method:

1. Chill mixer bowl, whisks and scraper for 10 minutes in the refrigerator.
2. Pour heavy cream into chilled mixer bowl fitted with the whisks and scraper.
3. Add both pieces of the lid then set timer to 5 minutes (mixing time might be shorter).
4. Mix on speed 5 until medium-stiff peaks form then set aside.
5. In a separate bowl, stir together the pumpkin puree, sugar, pumpkin spice, salt, vanilla and butter extract until sugar is dissolved then gently fold in the whipped cream.
6. Place a spoonful of cookie crumbs into the bottom of 8 dessert dishes.
7. Layer mousse and crumbs in dessert dishes to the top then sprinkle with additional crumbs.
8. Garnish with candy corn and gingerbread cookies before serving cold.

TIP

This dessert looks great served inside hollowed-out (steamed) mini pumpkins.

BULLSEYE CHEESECAKE

Makes 8 servings

Ingredients:

1/4 cup vanilla cookie crumbs

2 pounds (four 8-ounce packages) cream cheese, softened

1 cup granulated sugar

6 large eggs

1 teaspoon vanilla extract

2 squares unsweetened chocolate, melted

Method:

1. *Place a large pan or skillet with 1-inch of water in the oven then preheat to 300°F.*
2. *Wrap exterior of an 8-inch springform pan with aluminum foil then apply nonstick baking spray to the pan's interior then scatter with cookie crumbs.*
3. *Fit mixer with paddles and scraper then add cream cheese and sugar.*
4. *Add outer lid then set timer to 10 minutes.*
5. *Mix on speed 3 for 2-3 minutes, pause to see if additional scraping is necessary then continue mixing for an additional 5 minutes or until smooth.*
6. *Reduce to speed 3, add eggs and vanilla then mix just until blended thoroughly. Remove bowl then divide mixture between two separate bowls.*
7. *Whisk melted chocolate into one bowl until smooth.*
8. *Pour about 1/3 of dark mixture into the center of the prepared springform pan.*
9. *Repeat with white mixture poured directly into center of the pan.*
10. *Repeat with chocolate and white mixture until all is used. The bullseye rings will form by themselves through this pouring method.*
11. *Carefully place springform pan inside large pan or skillet with water in the oven.*
12. *Bake for 90 minutes, rotating pan halfway through baking (cover cake loosely with aluminum foil if it is darkening too much). To test for doneness, cake should jiggle when tapped but not ripple and internal temperature should be 155°F on a thermometer.*
13. *Remove from oven and let cool for 1 hour then wrap and chill for a minimum of 1 day or up to 5 days.*
14. *Serve cold.*

TIP

To neatly slice this cake, hold unflavored dental floss tightly between your hands then press floss down onto cake. When you reach the bottom, release one end of the floss and pull it through. Wipe floss and repeat until cut into desired slices.

STRAWBERRY DESSERT "LASAGNA"

Makes 10 servings

Ingredients:

24 golden crème sandwich cookies

1/2 cup unsalted butter, softened

2 cups whole milk ricotta cheese

Zest of 1 lemon

1/2 cup granulated sugar

3 cups strawberries, sliced

3 cups heavy cream, very cold

1 cup powdered sugar

1/2 teaspoon vanilla extract

1 cup white chocolate, shaved

Method:

1. *Place mixer bowl and whisks in refrigerator to chill.*
2. *Place cookies and butter into a food processor and pulse until crumbly.*
3. *Press cookie mixture into a firm layer inside a 9x13-inch pan; set aside.*
4. *Place ricotta, lemon zest and sugar into the food processor and process until smooth.*
5. *Fold sliced strawberries and ricotta together then spread over cookie layer.*
6. *Fit mixer with chilled bowl and whisks (no scraper) then add cream, powdered sugar and vanilla.*
7. *Add both pieces of the lid then set timer to 5 minutes (mixing time might be shorter).*
8. *Mix on speed 5 until stiff peaks form.*
9. *Spread whipped cream over ricotta layer in the pan.*
10. *Chill for 2 hours then top with white chocolate.*
11. *Cut into squares and serve.*

PEANUT BUTTER & JELLY COOKIES

Makes 4 dozen cookies

Ingredients:

1 cup smooth peanut butter

1/2 cup unsalted butter, softened

1/2 cup light brown sugar, packed

1/4 cup granulated sugar

1 large egg

1 teaspoon vanilla extract

1/4 teaspoon kosher salt

1 teaspoon baking soda

1 cup all purpose flour

Additional granulated sugar, for rolling

Tart cherry jam, for centers

Method:

1. *Preheat oven to 325°F and line two sheet pans with parchment paper; set aside.*
2. *Fit mixer with paddles and scraper then add peanut butter, butter and both sugars.*
3. *Add lid then set timer to 6 minutes (mixing time might be shorter).*
4. *Mix on speed 3 for 3 minutes then add egg and vanilla just until incorporated.*
5. *Pause mixer then add salt, baking soda and flour.*
6. *Set to speed 1 and mix just until incorporated.*
7. *Scoop up dough in 2-teaspoon size bits then roll into balls.*
8. *Roll each ball in additional sugar then place on sheet pans.*
9. *Use your thumb or index finger to make a well in the center of each cookie.*
10. *Bake for 12-18 minutes or until slightly puffed and brown.*
11. *Remove and let cool completely.*
12. *Fill centers with cherry jam just before serving.*

TIP

For a gluten-free version, swap the flour for a cup of your favorite gluten-free flour.

CHEDDAR BACON JALAPEÑO BREAD

Makes 1 loaf

Ingredients:

For the Dough

1 cup water

2 tablespoons olive oil

1 tablespoon rapid rise yeast

1/4 cup powdered milk

1/4 teaspoon apple cider vinegar

1 tablespoon kosher salt

1 tablespoon honey

1 large egg

3 cups unbleached bread flour

For Mixing In

1 large egg yolk

1 cup sharp Cheddar cheese, cubed

5 bacon slices, cooked and crumbled

2 jalapeño peppers, sliced

RECIPES

TIP

If you want to make this recipe ahead of time, follow recipe step 1-7 but skip the rising time. Wrap the pan well then freeze for up to 1 month. To bake, let loaf thaw for 4-6 hours or until 1-inch above the pan then bake following the recipe instructions.

Method:

1. *Fit mixer with the dough hook and pusher attachment then add all dough ingredients in the order listed.*
2. *Add lid then set timer to 10 minutes.*
3. *Mix on speed 2 until time is complete.*
4. *Remove dough hook attachment then cover and let dough rise for 1 hour or until doubled in bulk.*
5. *Transfer dough to a cutting board then top with all mix-in ingredients.*
6. *Use a bench scraper or chef's knife to chop ingredients into dough until dough and ingredients are in rough, irregular pieces.*
7. *Apply nonstick baking spray to a large loaf pan then scoop dough mixture into loaf pan and cover loosely with a towel; let rise for 40 minutes.*
8. *Preheat oven to 350°F then bake in lower third of oven for 40-50 minutes or until well-browned and internal temperature registers 195°F on a thermometer.*
9. *Remove and serve hot.*

OATMEAL CHOCOLATE CHIP COOKIES

Makes 18 cookies

Ingredients:

1 cup unsalted butter

1 cup granulated sugar

1 cup light brown sugar, packed

2 large eggs

2 teaspoons vanilla extract

1 1/2 cups all purpose flour

3 cups old fashioned rolled oats

1/2 teaspoon baking powder

1/2 teaspoon kosher salt

1 cup raisins

2 cups chocolate chips

Method:

1. Preheat oven to 325°F and cover two sheet pans with parchment paper; set aside.
2. Fit mixer with the paddles and scraper then add butter and both sugars.
3. Add outer lid then set timer to 5 minutes.
4. Mix on speed 4 for 4 minutes.
5. Reduce to speed 1 then add remaining ingredients in the order listed and mix just until combined.
6. Scoop up dough in 2-tablespoon bits then roll into balls and place on sheet pans 2-inches apart.
7. Bake for 10-12 minutes or until golden brown.
8. Remove and let slightly cool before serving.

MULTIGRAIN BREAD

Makes 1 loaf

Ingredients:

1 1/3 cups water

2 tablespoons olive oil

1 tablespoon rapid rise yeast

1 tablespoon soy sauce

2 tablespoons powdered milk

4 teaspoons vital wheat gluten (optional)

1 tablespoon kosher salt

1 tablespoon granulated sugar

1 cup store-bought multigrain blend + more for exterior

3 cups unbleached bread flour

Method:

1. *Fit mixer with the dough hook and pusher attachment then add all ingredients in the order listed.*
2. *Add lid then set timer to 10 minutes.*
3. *Mix on speed 2 until time is complete.*
4. *Remove dough hook attachment then cover and let rise for 1 hour or until doubled in bulk.*
5. *Apply nonstick baking spray to a large loaf pan.*
6. *Pat dough into a rectangle then roll up in a jelly roll fashion.*
7. *Brush loaf with some water then roll in additional multigrain blend.*
8. *Place seam-side down into the loaf pan then cover and let rise for 40 minutes.*
9. *Place oven rack in lower third of oven then preheat to 350°F.*
10. *Bake loaf in the lower third of the oven for 40-50 minutes or until well-browned and internal temperature registers 195°F on a thermometer.*
11. *Remove and let cool before serving.*

EASY FRUIT COBBLER

Makes 6-8 servings

Ingredients:

For the Pan

2 tablespoons unsalted butter, softened

2 tablespoons granulated sugar

For the Cobbler

1/2 cup unsalted butter, softened

1 1/4 cups self-rising flour

1 can (14 ounces) sweetened condensed milk

1/2 cup whole milk

1 tablespoon vanilla extract

3 cups fruit of your choice, divided

1/4 cup granulated sugar, for topping

Method:

1. *Preheat oven to 350°F then butter and sugar a 9x13-inch pan; set aside.*
2. *Fit mixer with whisks (no scraper) then add the butter, flour, condensed milk, whole milk and vanilla.*
3. *Add lid then set timer to 3 minutes.*
4. *Mix on speed 3 until time is complete.*
5. *Spoon mixture into prepared pan then gently smooth the top.*
6. *Scatter half of the fruit over the top.*
7. *Bake for 20 minutes (the fruit will sink to the bottom of the pan during baking).*
8. *Top with remaining fruit, sprinkle with sugar then bake for an additional 15 minutes or until well browned.*
9. *Remove and serve hot.*

LEMON
POUND CAKE

Makes 1 loaf

Ingredients:

For the Cake

3/4 cup (1 1/2 sticks) unsalted butter, softened

4 ounces (1/2 cup) cream cheese, softened

1 1/2 cups granulated sugar

3 large eggs

Zest from 2 lemons

2 tablespoons fresh lemon juice

1 teaspoon kosher salt

1/4 teaspoon ground turmeric (optional)

1 1/2 cups unbleached all purpose flour

1 teaspoon baking powder

For the Glaze

1 2/3 cups powdered sugar

Zest from 2 lemons

2 tablespoons fresh lemon juice

1 tablespoon heavy cream

Method:

1. *Preheat oven to 350°F and apply nonstick baking spray to a loaf pan; set aside.*
2. *Fit mixer with paddles and scraper then add butter, cream cheese and sugar.*
3. *Add lid then set timer to 8 minutes.*
4. *Mix on speed 3 until time is complete.*
5. *Add eggs, zest and lemon juice then mix on speed 2 for 1 minute.*
6. *Add remaining cake ingredients and mix on speed 1 just until combined.*
7. *Spoon batter into prepared pan.*
8. *Bake for 1 hour or until brown and a wooden pick inserted in the center emerges clean.*
9. *While cake bakes, stir together all glaze ingredients in a small bowl.*
10. *When baking is complete, remove cake and let cool for 30 minutes.*
11. *Place on a serving plate and spoon glaze over top of cake.*
12. *Serve warm.*

CHEESE SOUFFLÉ

Makes 4 servings

Ingredients:

1/3 cup grated Parmesan cheese + more for ramekins

4 large egg yolks

1 cup Gruyere cheese, shredded

1/2 cup cream cheese, softened

1/3 cup whole milk

1/2 teaspoon dry mustard

1/4 teaspoon kosher salt

1/8 teaspoon freshly ground black pepper

2 green onions, roughly chopped

4 large egg whites

A pinch of cream of tartar

Method:

1. *Preheat oven to 350°F and apply nonstick baking spray to four large ramekins.*
2. *Sprinkle the bottom and sides of ramekins with Parmesan cheese then place on a sheet pan; set aside.*
3. *Place all ingredients, except egg whites and cream of tartar, into a blender.*
4. *Blend on high speed for 30 seconds or until smooth.*
5. *Fit clean mixer with clean whisks (no scraper) then add egg whites.*
6. *Add outer lid then set timer to 4 minutes.*
7. *Mix on speed 3 for 30 seconds then add cream of tartar.*
8. *Increase to speed 5 and mix to medium peaks.*
9. *Fold mixture from blender into egg whites using a spatula until uniform then divide between ramekins filling them almost to the top.*
10. *Bake in center of the oven for 30 minutes or until well risen and brown.*
11. *Remove and serve immediately before they start to deflate.*

RECIPES

BASIC WHITE BREAD

Makes 1 loaf

Ingredients:

1 cup water

2 tablespoons olive oil

1 tablespoon rapid rise yeast

1/4 cup powdered milk

1/4 teaspoon apple cider vinegar

1 tablespoon kosher salt

1 tablespoon honey

1 large egg

3 cups unbleached bread flour

Method:

1. *Fit mixer with the dough hook and pusher attachment then add all ingredients in the order listed.*
2. *Add lid then set timer to 10 minutes.*
3. *Mix on speed 2 until time is complete.*
4. *Remove dough hook attachment then cover and let rise for 1 hour or until doubled in bulk.*
5. *Apply nonstick baking spray to a large loaf pan.*
6. *Remove dough, pat into a rectangle then roll up in a jelly roll fashion.*
7. *Place roll in pan, seam-side down, then cover loosely with a towel and let rise for 40 minutes.*
8. *Preheat oven to 350°F and bake in lower third of oven for 40-50 minutes until well-browned and internal temperature registers 195°F on a thermometer.*
9. *Remove and serve warm.*

TIP

If you prefer a softer crust, brush melted butter all over loaf shortly after it comes out of the oven.

DATE OAT ENERGY BITES

Makes 24 balls

Ingredients:

12 Medjool dates, pitted and quartered

2/3 cup almond butter, warmed

Zest from 1 orange (optional)

1 1/4 cups old fashioned rolled oats + more for rolling

2 tablespoons cocoa powder

1/3 cup sesame seeds

2 tablespoons flax seeds

2 teaspoons vanilla extract

Method:

1. *Fit mixer with paddles (no scraper) then add all ingredients.*
2. *Add lid then set timer to 8 minutes.*
3. *Mix on speed 1 for 1 minute then speed 2 for 7 minutes.*
4. *When mixing is complete, roll mixture into 1 tablespoon size balls using additional oats to prevent sticking.*
5. *Let rest at room temperature for 2 hours.*
6. *Place in airtight container and store in the refrigerator for up to 1 month.*

TIP

If your dates are dry and hard, cut them into small bits and add 1 tablespoon of water or coconut oil to the ingredients.

LAVA CAKE

Makes 6 cakes

Ingredients:

10 ounces bittersweet chocolate pieces

1 1/4 cups unsalted butter

1/2 cup all purpose flour or cornstarch

6 large eggs

1 cup granulated sugar

1/2 cup crunchy peanut butter

1/2 cup marshmallow crème

Powdered sugar, for serving

Strawberries, for serving

Method:

1. Preheat oven to 350°F and generously apply nonstick baking spray to six ramekins; set aside.
2. Combine chocolate and butter in a microwave-safe bowl then microwave until melted and fluid.
3. Whisk flour or cornstarch into the melted chocolate mixture.
4. Fit mixer with whisks and scraper then add eggs and sugar.
5. Add outer lid then set timer to 8 minutes.
6. Mix on speed 5 until quadrupled in volume and satiny.
7. Stop mixer then pour chocolate mixture into mixer and quickly resume mixing on speed 5 for just a few seconds until mostly uniform in color.
8. Remove whisks and use a spatula to ensure that all the chocolate is incorporated evenly.
9. Pour mixture into ramekins, filling them almost to the top.
10. Top each with a spoonful of peanut butter and marshmallow crème.
11. Cover with a bit more chocolate mixture.
12. Place in oven and bake for 15-20 minutes or until slightly domed.
13. Remove from oven and invert onto serving plates, tapping ramekins to release cakes if necessary.
14. Top with powdered sugar and strawberries before serving.

TIP

To make these for serving at a later time, assemble completely
then wrap and freeze until solid. Store frozen for up to 3 months.
To serve, bake from a frozen state for 30-35 minutes.

JALAPEÑO CORNBREAD

Makes 6 servings

Ingredients:

2 large eggs

1 1/4 cups buttermilk

1/2 cup unsalted butter, melted

1/2 cup frozen corn kernels

2 jalapeño peppers, sliced + more for topping

1 bunch green onions, chopped

1/2 cup Cheddar cheese, shredded + more for topping

2 teaspoons kosher salt

1 cup all purpose flour

1 cup yellow cornmeal

1 tablespoon granulated sugar

Method:

1. Preheat oven to 375°F and apply nonstick baking spray to an 8-inch square pan; set aside.
2. Fit mixer with whisks (no scraper) then add all ingredients.
3. Add lid then set timer to 3 minutes.
4. Mix on speed 3 until time is complete then pour mixture into prepared pan.
5. Top with additional jalapeño peppers and Cheddar cheese.
6. Bake for 25-30 minutes or until well browned and a wooden pick inserted in the center emerges clean.
7. Remove and serve hot.

BUFFALO CHICKEN
MINI BOATS

Makes 12 mini boats

Ingredients:

1 package (12-count) fiesta flat taco shells

1/2 cup Parmesan cheese, grated

1/4 cup blue cheese crumbles

1 package (8 ounces) cream cheese, softened

1 bunch green onions, sliced

1/2 cup bottled wing sauce + more for brushing

Kosher salt and fresh pepper to taste

2 cups leftover rotisserie chicken, chopped

1 cup canned French fried onions

1/2 cup celery, diced

Method:

1. Preheat oven to 375°F and place taco shells on a sheet pan.
2. Brush taco shells with wing sauce.
3. Fit mixer with paddles and scraper then add Parmesan, blue cheese, cream cheese, green onions and wing sauce.
4. Add lid then set timer to 5 minutes.
5. Mix on speed 4 until time is complete.
6. Add salt, pepper, chicken and fried onions.
7. Set timer to 1 minute and mix on speed 2 until time is complete.
8. When mixing is complete spoon mixture into taco shells.
9. Bake for 12-15 minutes or until heated through.
10. Remove, top with celery and serve hot.

PECAN MASHED
SWEET POTATOES

Makes 6 servings

Ingredients:

For the Topping

1 cup pecan pieces

3 tablespoons unsalted butter

2 tablespoons granulated sugar

A pinch of kosher salt

For the Potatoes

5 pounds sweet potatoes, peeled and quartered

Kosher salt to taste

3 tablespoons light brown sugar, packed

4 tablespoons unsalted butter

1/2 teaspoon vanilla extract

1/2 cup cream + more as desired

Method:

1. *In a large skillet over medium heat, add the pecans, butter, sugar and salt.*
2. *Stir constantly until brown and fragrant then set aside to cool and break apart.*
3. *Place sweet potatoes and salt in a stockpot then add cold water until potatoes are covered by 1-inch of water.*
4. *Bring to a boil over high heat then lower heat to a gentle simmer.*
5. *Boil for 20 minutes or until fork tender.*
6. *Drain thoroughly then return to heat for an additional 1 minute to dry off excess water.*
7. *Fit mixer with whisks (no scraper) then add potatoes, salt and brown sugar.*
8. *Add outer lid then set timer to 2 minutes.*
9. *Mix on speed 4 just until chunks are broken up.*
10. *Add butter, vanilla and cream then mix on speed 1 until desired texture is achieved.*
11. *Transfer to a serving bowl then top with cooled pecan mixture before serving hot.*

SPINACH ARTICHOKE

Makes 8 servings

Ingredients:

1 cup Parmesan cheese, grated

1/4 cup feta cheese, crumbled

1 package (8 ounces) cream cheese, softened

1 bunch green onions, sliced

6 garlic cloves, minced

2 tablespoons light miso paste (optional)

1 can (12 ounces) artichoke hearts, drained

1/2 cup mayonnaise

2 tablespoons capers (optional)

Kosher salt and fresh pepper to taste

6 cups fresh spinach

1 cup panko bread crumbs

Assorted dippers of your choice

Method:

1. Preheat oven to 350°F then butter a 2-quart baking dish; set aside.
2. Fit mixer with paddles and scraper then add Parmesan, feta, cream cheese, green onions and garlic.
3. Add lid then set timer to 5 minutes.
4. Mix on speed 4 until time is complete.
5. Add miso, artichokes, mayonnaise, capers if using, salt, pepper and spinach.
6. Set timer to 1 minute and mix on speed 2 until time is complete.
7. Spoon mixture into prepared baking dish then smooth top.
8. Top with panko and bake for 25 minutes or until brown and bubbly.
9. Remove and serve hot with dippers of your choice.

OLIVER'S GLUTEN-FREE
BRIOCHE

Makes 1 loaf

Ingredients:

1 1/4 cups water

2 tablespoons granulated sugar

1 tablespoon rapid rise yeast

4 egg yolks

1/2 cup powdered milk

1/2 teaspoon apple cider vinegar

3 1/2 cups gluten-free flour

2 teaspoons kosher salt

5 tablespoons unsalted butter + for brushing

Method:

1. *Fit mixer with the paddles and scraper then add all ingredients in the order listed.*
2. *Add lid then set timer to 10 minutes.*
3. *Mix on speed 3 until time is complete.*
4. *While batter is mixing, apply nonstick baking spray to a large loaf pan.*
5. *When mixing is complete, pour mixture into loaf pan then smooth the top.*
6. *Cover and let rise for 45 minutes.*
7. *Preheat oven to 350°F and bake in the lower third of the oven for 40-50 minutes or until internal temperature registers 195°F on a thermometer.*
8. *Remove then brush finished loaf with additional butter before serving warm.*

WOLFGANG'S FAVORITE
COOKIES

Makes 4 dozen cookies

Ingredients:

1 cup unsalted butter, softened

1/4 cup light brown sugar, packed

1 1/2 cups toasted hazelnuts, chopped

1 1/2 cups all purpose flour

1/2 teaspoon kosher salt

1 teaspoon vanilla extract

Granulated sugar, for rolling

Method:

1. Preheat oven to 350°F.
2. Line two large sheet pans with parchment paper.
3. Fit mixer with the paddles and scraper then add butter and brown sugar.
4. Add outer lid then set timer to 6 minutes.
5. Mix on speed 4 until time is complete.
6. Add hazelnuts then set mixer to speed 2 and mix just until combined.
7. Reduce to speed 1 while adding remaining ingredients, except granulated sugar, and mix just until no dry flour remains (do not over mix).
8. Use a small ice cream scoop or teaspoon to drop small mounds of dough onto the sheet pans (these cookies do not spread much).
9. Bake 25-30 minutes or until deep brown and fragrant.
10. Remove from oven then roll cookies in granulated sugar (be gentle as cookies are tender).
11. Let cool for a few minutes before transferring to a serving plate.

NO CHURN
CHERRY ICE CREAM

Makes 6 servings

Ingredients:

3 cups heavy cream

1 can (14 ounces) sweetened condensed milk

1 1/2 cups canned cherry pie filling

1/4 cup almonds, chopped

Method:

1. *Fit mixer with whisks and scraper then add the heavy cream.*
2. *Add both pieces of the lid then set timer to 3 minutes (mixing time might be shorter).*
3. *Mix on speed 5 for 2 minutes or until soft peaks form then pause mixer.*
4. *Add remaining ingredients then mix on speed 3 for the remaining 1 minute or until blended.*
5. *Scrape mixture into a freezer-safe container then freeze for a minimum of 3 hours or until solid.*
6. *Scoop and serve as desired.*

TIP

To make other flavors, use any other canned pie filling instead of the cherry pie filling. You can also skip the pie filling and make vanilla ice cream by adding 2 teaspoons vanilla extract or make chocolate ice cream by whisking in 1/3 cup cocoa powder.

OLD FASHIONED BLUEBERRY COFFEE CAKE

Makes 12 servings

Ingredients:

For the Cake

1 cup unsalted butter, softened

1 1/4 cups light brown sugar, packed

3 large eggs

1 cup whole milk

2 cups all purpose flour

1 tablespoon baking powder

1 teaspoon kosher salt

1 tablespoon cornstarch

1/2 cup fresh blueberries

For the Topping

1/4 cup granulated sugar

1/2 teaspoon ground cinnamon

1/2 cup fresh blueberries

Method:

1. Preheat oven to 350°F and apply nonstick baking spray to a 9x13-inch pan; set aside.
2. Fit mixer with paddles (no scraper) then add butter, sugar and eggs.
3. Add outer lid then set timer to 5 minutes.
4. Mix on speed 4 for 4 minutes.
5. Reduce to speed 1, add milk, flour, baking powder and salt then mix for 1 minute.
6. Toss cornstarch and blueberries together then fold into batter using a rubber spatula.
7. Spoon batter into prepared 9x13-inch pan.
8. In a separate mixing bowl, stir together all topping ingredients then scatter over the batter.
9. Bake for 45-50 minutes or until a wooden pick inserted in the center comes out clean.
10. Remove and serve warm.

CRINKLE COOKIES

Makes 24 cookies

Ingredients:

1/2 cup vegetable oil

4 large eggs

2 cups granulated sugar

1 cup cocoa powder

2 teaspoons vanilla extract

1 teaspoon kosher salt

2 teaspoons baking powder

2 cups all purpose flour

Additional granulated sugar, for rolling

Powdered sugar, for rolling

Method:

1. *Preheat oven to 350°F and line two sheet pans with parchment paper; set aside.*
2. *Fit mixer with paddles and scraper then add oil, eggs and sugar.*
3. *Add lid then set timer to 5 minutes.*
4. *Mix on speed 3 until time is complete.*
5. *Reduce to speed 1, set timer to 2 minutes then add cocoa, vanilla, salt, baking powder and flour.*
6. *Mix just until uniform in color.*
7. *Scoop up dough in 2-tablespoon bits then roll into balls.*
8. *Roll each ball in granulated sugar followed by powdered sugar until thoroughly coated.*
9. *Place on prepared sheet pans and space out evenly.*
10. *Bake for 15 minutes or until puffed and cracked.*
11. *Remove and serve warm.*

MELTED SNOWMAN
CUPCAKES

Makes 12 cupcakes

Ingredients:

1 cup unsalted butter, softened

3 cups light brown sugar, packed

4 large eggs

1 tablespoon vanilla extract

2/3 cup quality cocoa powder

2 teaspoons baking soda

1/2 teaspoon kosher salt

2 cups cake flour

1 1/2 cups sour cream

1 1/3 cups water

Really Easy Buttercream (see recipe on page 18)

1 cup powdered sugar

Large marshmallows

Cinnamon candies

Food coloring as desired

Method:

1. Preheat oven to 350°F and line a cupcake pan with cupcake liners.
2. Fit mixer with whisks and scraper then add butter and sugar.
3. Add outer lid then set timer to 8 minutes.
4. Mix on speed 3 for 4 minutes or until butter is fluffy.
5. Add eggs and vanilla then mix on speed 3 until uniform.
6. Reduce to speed 1 then add cocoa, baking soda, salt and flour; mix until color is uniform.
7. Add sour cream and water then mix until smooth.
8. Fill cupcake liners 3/4 full of batter.
9. Bake for about 20 minutes or until domed and set then remove and let cool.
10. In a small bowl, stir 1/4 cup buttercream into the powdered sugar.
11. Mix until a fondant-like texture is achieved then color orange and form "carrot" noses.
12. Color a small amount of buttercream black then transfer to a small piping bag.
13. Frost each cupcake with white buttercream to look like melting snow then add a marshmallow head.
14. Attach a nose to each marshmallow head using a dot of buttercream as "glue".
15. Use black buttercream to pipe eyes, mouths and arms, blue buttercream for scarves as well as red and green buttercream for holly.
16. Press 3 cinnamon candy buttons on each snowman before serving.

TIP

To make these cupcakes look "melty", microwave the buttercream for just a few seconds then stir thoroughly before frosting the cupcakes. Pile the frosting a bit higher under the marshmallow so that it looks like the snowman is in the process of melting.

CHOCOLATE CACTUS CUPCAKES

Makes 12 cupcakes

Ingredients:

1 teaspoon kosher salt

1 teaspoon baking powder

2 teaspoons baking soda

1 cup cocoa powder

2 cups granulated sugar

1 3/4 cups all purpose flour

1 cup regular buttermilk (not low-fat)

1/2 cup vegetable oil

2 large eggs

2 teaspoons vanilla extract

1/2 cup milk

Really Easy Buttercream (see recipe on page 18)

Graham cracker crumbs

Food coloring as desired

Method:

1. *Preheat oven to 350°F and apply nonstick baking spray to a 12-spot cupcake pan; set aside.*
2. *Fit mixer with whisks and scraper then add all ingredients, except buttercream, cracker crumbs and food coloring.*
3. *Add lid then set timer to 3 minutes.*
4. *Mix on speed 4 until time is complete.*
5. *Divide batter evenly between cupcake wells until each is 2/3 full then bake for 20-22 minutes or until a wooden pick inserted off-center comes out with just a few moist crumbs clinging to it.*
6. *Let cool completely.*
7. *Apply a thin layer of buttercream to the top of each cupcake then dip in cracker crumbs.*
8. *Mix different shades of green buttercream then add a bit of black food coloring to make dusky hues if desired. Pipe various cacti on top of cupcakes using a pastry bag and a variety of tips.*

TIP

To make the cupcakes look as pictured, bake the cupcakes in small terra-cotta flowerpots available a many cake decorating stores.

MOCHA FUDGE BROWNIES

Makes 9 servings

Ingredients:

2 teaspoons instant coffee

1 cup unsalted butter, softened

2 cups granulated sugar

4 large eggs

1/4 teaspoon kosher salt

1 teaspoon vanilla extract

1/2 cup good quality cocoa

1 cup unbleached all purpose flour

1 jar (10 ounces) fudge topping

Method:

1. Preheat oven to 350°F and apply nonstick baking spray to a 9x9-inch pan; set aside.
2. Fit mixer with paddles and scraper then add coffee, butter and sugar.
3. Add lid then set timer to 6 minutes.
4. Mix on speed 4 until time is complete.
5. Add eggs and mix on speed 3 for 1 minute.
6. Add remaining ingredients, except fudge, then mix on speed 1 for 1 minute.
7. Spoon into prepared pan then smooth the top.
8. Bake for 1 hour or until a wooden pick inserted off-center emerges clean.
9. Let cool completely then add fudge topping before serving.

BROILED OATMEAL CAKE

Makes 1 cake

Ingredients:

For the Cake

1 cup quick-cooking oats

1 cup hot water

1/2 cup unsalted butter, softened

2 cups light brown sugar, packed

2 large eggs

2 teaspoons vanilla extract

1 1/2 cups all purpose flour

1 teaspoon baking soda

1 teaspoon ground cinnamon

1/2 teaspoon ground nutmeg

1/2 teaspoon kosher salt

For the Topping

1/4 cup unsalted butter

3/4 cup light brown sugar, packed

1/4 cup heavy cream or milk

1 1/3 cups sweetened coconut, shredded

Method:

1. *In a small bowl, mix together oats and hot water then let stand for 5 minutes.*
2. *Preheat oven to 350°F and apply nonstick baking spray to a 9x13-inch pan; set aside.*
3. *Fit mixer with whisks and scraper then add soaked oats mixture, butter, sugar, eggs and vanilla.*
4. *Add lid then set timer to 4 minutes.*
5. *Mix on speed 4 for 3 minutes.*
6. *Add remaining cake ingredients then mix on speed 1 for remaining 1 minute.*
7. *Spoon mixture into prepared 9x13-inch pan and bake for 30-35 minutes or until brown and a wooden pick inserted off-center comes out with just a few moist crumbs clinging to it.*
8. *Remove and preheat broiler.*
9. *Combine all topping ingredients in a microwave-safe bowl, microwave until bubbly then spread over cake.*
10. *Broil for 2-3 minutes or until brown and bubbly then remove and serve warm.*

TIP

If you only have old fashioned oats instead of the quick-cooking kind, simply add 2 extra tablespoons water to the oat/water mixture then microwave until a full boil is achieved before proceeding with the recipe.

GRANDMA'S MEATBALLS

Makes 24 meatballs

Ingredients:

3 white bread slices, torn into bits

1/3 cup whole milk

1 pound ground beef

1 pound ground pork

2 large eggs

1/2 cup ketchup

2 tablespoons soy sauce

1 medium yellow onion, finely chopped

1/2 cup whole milk ricotta cheese

1/2 teaspoon dried sage

Kosher salt and fresh pepper to taste

1 tablespoon brown sugar, packed

Chopped parsley, for serving

Method:

1. *Preheat oven to 375°F and line a large sheet pan with aluminum foil; set aside.*
2. *Fit mixer with dough hook and pusher attachment then add the bread and milk.*
3. *Stir bread occasionally for 3 minutes or until all the milk is absorbed then add remaining ingredients, except parsley.*
4. *Add lid then set time to 2 minutes (mixing time might be shorter).*
5. *Mix on speed 1 just until combined and scrape bowl if necessary.*
6. *Roll mixture into 24 balls using gloves and a bit of water to prevent sticking.*
7. *Arrange meatballs evenly on the prepared sheet pan.*
8. *Bake for 20-25 minutes or until well browned and internal temperature registers 165°F on a meat thermometer.*
9. *Remove, garnish with parsley and serve.*

BBQ CHICKEN CHEESY BREAD

Makes 1 loaf

Ingredients:

1 store-bought Italian bread loaf

1 package (8 ounces) cream cheese, softened

1/2 cup mayonnaise

1/2 cup bottled BBQ sauce

Kosher salt and fresh pepper to taste

2 cups leftover rotisserie chicken, chopped

8 Provolone cheese slices

Method:

1. *Preheat oven to 375°F.*
2. *Cut top off the bread loaf then hollow out until a 1-inch border remains; set aside.*
3. *Fit mixer with paddles and scraper then add cream cheese, mayonnaise, BBQ sauce, salt and pepper.*
4. *Add lid then set timer to 4 minutes.*
5. *Mix on speed 4 until time is complete.*
6. *Fold chicken into cream cheese mixture using a spatula then scrape into bread loaf.*
7. *Cover top with cheese slices then place bread loaf on a sheet pan.*
8. *Bake for 20-25 minutes or until brown and bubbly.*
9. *Remove, let cool for 5 minutes then slice and serve.*

CARROT RAISIN BREAD

Makes 1 loaf

Ingredients:

2 cups carrots, finely shredded

1/2 cup (1 stick) unsalted butter, softened

1 cup granulated sugar

2 large eggs

1 teaspoon vanilla extract

3 tablespoons sour cream

1/2 cup raisins

2 cups unbleached all purpose flour

1 teaspoon baking soda

1/2 teaspoon baking powder

1/2 teaspoon kosher salt

1 teaspoon ground cinnamon

Method:

1. Preheat oven to 350°F and apply nonstick baking spray to a loaf pan.
2. Fit mixer with whisks and scraper then add the carrots, butter and sugar.
3. Add outer lid then set timer to 8 minutes.
4. Mix on speed 4 for 4 minutes then pause the mixer.
5. Add eggs, vanilla and sour cream then mix on speed 3 for 3 minutes.
6. Pause mixer then add remaining ingredients and mix on speed 1 until time is complete.
7. Pour batter into prepared loaf pan.
8. Bake for 50-60 minutes or until well browned and a wooden pick inserted off-center comes out with just a few moist crumbs clinging to it.
9. Let cool for 20-30 minutes before removing from pan.
10. Serve warm.

MASHED POTATO "FROSTED" MEATLOAF

Makes 6 servings

Ingredients:

Bacon Wrapped Meatloaf (see recipe on page 20)

Mashed Potatoes (see recipe on page 12)

1 large egg, beaten

Kosher salt and fresh pepper to taste

Chives, chopped, for serving

Method:

1. Preheat oven to 375°F.
2. "Frost" meatloaf with a thick layer of mashed potatoes.
3. Brush mashed potatoes with the beaten egg then sprinkle with salt and pepper.
4. Bake for 20-25 minutes or until potatoes are browned and hot.
5. Remove, garnish with chives and serve hot.

TIP

As an alternative, use the Mashed Sweet Potatoes from the recipe on page 46 without the nut topping instead of the white mashed potatoes in this recipe.

TOMATO FOCACCIA

Makes 8-10 squares

Ingredients:

1 2/3 cups water

4 tablespoons olive oil + more for pan and top

1 tablespoon rapid rise yeast

2 tablespoons honey

3 tablespoons tomato paste

1 tablespoon paprika

3 cups unbleached bread flour

1 tablespoon kosher salt + more for top

A handful of fresh oregano sprigs

2 cups cherry tomatoes, whole or halved

Method:

1. *In the mixer bowl, stir together the water, oil, yeast, honey and tomato paste using a spoon then let rest for 5 minutes.*
2. *Fit mixer with the dough hook and pusher attachment then add paprika, flour and salt on top of water mixture in the mixer bowl.*
3. *Add lid then set timer to 10 minutes.*
4. *Mix on speed 3 until time is complete (mixture will be soft).*
5. *Scrape bowl as needed.*
6. *Remove dough hook attachment then cover and let rise for 30 minutes or until doubled in bulk.*
7. *Generously oil a 1/2 sheet pan then pour dough batter onto sheet pan; smooth to edges then let rise for an additional 30 minutes.*
8. *Preheat oven to 425°F.*
9. *Drizzle top with additional oil, scatter with oregano and tomatoes then dimple the top using your fingertips.*
10. *Sprinkle with additional salt then bake for 20-22 minutes or until well browned.*
11. *Remove, garnish as desired and serve hot.*

PIZZA DOUGH

Makes two 10-inch pizza crusts

Ingredients:

1 cup water

2 tablespoons olive oil

1 tablespoon rapid rise yeast

1 tablespoon honey

3 cups unbleached bread flour

1 tablespoon kosher salt

Method:

1. *Fit mixer with the dough hook and pusher attachment then add all ingredients in the order listed.*
2. *Add lid then set timer to 10 minutes.*
3. *Mix on speed 2 until time is complete.*
4. *Remove, cut dough in half then roll each piece into a tight ball.*
5. *Place balls seam-side down on an oiled pan.*
6. *Cover and let rise for 1 hour before using.*
7. *Dough can be frozen for up to 1 month.*

TIP

To bake a pizza, stretch dough out as desired, add your favorite toppings then bake in a very hot 500°F oven for 10-15 minutes or until brown and bubbly.

DULCE DE LECHE PIE

Makes 8 servings

Ingredients:

1 can (14 ounces) dulce de leche, warmed until fluid

1 store-bought graham cracker pie crust

2 packages (8 ounces each) cream cheese, softened

2 cups heavy whipping cream, cold

1/3 cup granulated sugar

2 teaspoons pure vanilla extract

Method:

1. *Drizzle half of the dulce de leche over the pie crust, spreading gently; set aside.*
2. *Fit mixer with whisks and scraper then add cream cheese and remaining dulce de leche.*
3. *Add lid then set timer to 2 minutes.*
4. *Mix on speed 4 until time is complete.*
5. *Spoon cream cheese mixture on top of dulce de leche in the crust then smooth the top.*
6. *Wash mixer bowl, whisks and scraper then reassemble and add cream, sugar and vanilla.*
7. *Add lid then set timer to 4 minutes (mixing time might be shorter).*
8. *Mix on speed 5 until stiff peaks form.*
9. *Spread whipped cream over the top of the cream cheese mixture in the crust.*
10. *Refrigerate for 1 hour, garnish as desired and serve.*

CINNAMON ROLLS

Makes 15 rolls

Ingredients:

For the Buns

1 cup whole milk

2 tablespoons vegetable oil

1 tablespoon rapid rise yeast

1 large egg

1/2 teaspoon apple cider vinegar

1 tablespoon honey

2 teaspoons kosher salt

1/2 cup powdered milk

3 cups all purpose flour

For the Filling

5 tablespoons unsalted butter, melted

1 teaspoon vanilla extract

1 cup light brown sugar, packed

1 tablespoon ground cinnamon

1/2 cup chopped pecans (optional)

Method:

1. *Fit mixer with dough hook and pusher attachment then add all bun ingredients.*
2. *Add lid then set timer to 10 minutes.*
3. *Mix on speed 2 until time is complete.*
4. *Remove dough hook attachment, cover and let rise for 40 minutes.*
5. *Roll out the dough into a 16x8-inch rectangle.*
6. *In a small bowl, stir together all filling ingredients using a spatula.*
7. *Spread dough with filling then roll up dough in a jelly roll fashion.*
8. *Pinch edges to seal then cut into 15 rolls.*
9. *Apply nonstick baking spray to a 9x13-inch pan then place rolls on prepared pan.*
10. *Cover and let rise for 30 minutes.*
11. *Preheat oven to 350°F.*
12. *Bake rolls for 30-35 minutes or until golden brown.*
13. *Remove rolls and serve warm.*

OLD FASHIONED
ANIMAL CRACKERS

Makes 6 dozen

Ingredients:

For the Crackers

1 1/2 cups unsalted butter

1 2/3 cups light brown sugar, packed

1 teaspoon butter extract

1 teaspoon vanilla extract

3 large eggs

1 teaspoon kosher salt

5 cups all purpose flour

For the Icing

3 tablespoons heavy cream

1/4 teaspoon lemon extract

2 cups powdered sugar

Food coloring as desired

Sprinkles (optional)

Method:

1. *Fit mixer with paddles and scraper then add butter, sugar and both extracts.*
2. *Add lid then set timer to 6 minutes.*
3. *Mix on speed 3 for 3 minutes.*
4. *Add eggs and mix until incorporated.*
5. *Reduce to speed 1 then add salt and flour; mix just until incorporated then remove and refrigerate dough for 2 hours.*
6. *Preheat oven to 350°F and line two sheet pans with parchment paper; set aside.*
7. *Roll out dough between two sheets of plastic wrap then cut out using animal-shaped cookie cutters and place on prepared sheet pans.*
8. *Bake for 10-12 minutes or until golden brown then remove and let cool.*
9. *Mix icing by stirring together the cream, lemon extract, powdered sugar and food coloring.*
10. *Use a pastry brush to brush a thin layer of icing over the top of each cookie.*
11. *Top with sprinkles if desired then let dry for 20 minutes before serving.*

TIP

The cookie cutters I use have a spring loaded center post that imprint designs on the cookies when pressed down. They are made from silicone which prevents the dough from sticking. See the source page 109 for online sources to purchase.

OLD FASHIONED
WHIPPED CREAM

Makes 4 cups

Ingredients:

2 cups heavy cream, very cold

1/3 cup granulated sugar

1/2 teaspoon vanilla extract

Method:

1. *Chill mixer bowl and whisks for 10 minutes in the refrigerator.*
2. *Fit mixer with chilled mixer bowl and whisks (no scraper) then add all ingredients.*
3. *Add both pieces of the lid then set timer to 5 minutes (mixing time might be shorter).*
4. *Mix on speed 5 until medium peaks form.*
5. *Use as desired.*

TIP

You will achieve better volume if you ensure that everything is very cold before mixing.

HOMEMADE
PIE CRUST

Makes two 9-inch pie crusts

Ingredients:

2 3/4 cups all purpose flour

1 cup unsalted butter, cold, cut into 1/2-inch pieces

1/3 cup granulated sugar

1/2 teaspoon kosher salt

3 large egg yolks

1/4 cup heavy cream

Method:

1. *Fit mixer with paddles and scraper then add flour, butter, sugar and salt.*
2. *In a separate small bowl, whisk together the egg yolks and cream; set aside.*
3. *Add outer lid then set timer to 2 minutes (mixing time might be less).*
4. *Mix on speed 3 for 30-40 seconds or just until the butter pieces are small.*
5. *Add cream mixture all at once, increase to speed 4 then mix for 10 seconds or just until no cream is visible.*
6. *Remove from the bowl then knead by hand and shape into two dough balls.*
7. *Wrap and chill for a minimum of 1 hour or up to 3 days before rolling out and using.*
8. *To bake a crust, roll out 1 dough ball (reserve other dough ball for later use) on a floured surface, fit into a greased pie pan then crimp edges.*
9. *Place a sheet of parchment paper over crust then fill pan to the top with dried beans or dried rice to weigh it down.*
10. *Bake at 350°F for 20-25 minutes or until edges are golden brown.*
11. *Remove and let cool before filling.*

LIMEADE FREEZER PIE

Makes one 8-inch pie

Ingredients:

1 package (3 ounces) lime-flavored gelatin

1/2 cup boiling water

1/2 cup granulated sugar

Zest and juice from 2 limes + more for serving

3 packages (8 ounces each) cream cheese, softened

1 store-bought graham cracker pie crust

Old Fashioned Whipped Cream (see recipe on page 70)

Method:

1. *In a small mixing bowl, combine the gelatin and boiling water then stir to dissolve.*
2. *Fit mixer with whisks and scraper then add gelatin mixture, sugar, lime zest and juice as well as cream cheese.*
3. *Add lid then set timer to 4 minutes.*
4. *Mix on speed 1 then gradually increase to speed 5 and mix until time is complete.*
5. *Pour mixture into pie crust then smooth top.*
6. *Freeze for a minimum of 2 hours or until firm to the touch.*
7. *Cover with whipped cream then garnish with lime zest and slices.*
8. *Serve semi-frozen.*

TRIPLE LAYERED CHOCOLATE TOWERS

Makes 9 towers

Ingredients:

Mocha Fudge Brownies (see recipe on page 57)

Chocolate Mousse (see recipe on page 83)

Old Fashioned Whipped Cream (see recipe on page 70)

Chocolate shavings, for garnish

Method:

1. *Cut out nine 2-inch circles from the brownies then place on a sheet pan.*
2. *Wrap each circle with a 3-inch tall strip of acetate, securing ends with tape.*
3. *Using a piping bag or a zipper top bag with one corner snipped off, add a layer of mousse to each tower.*
4. *Using a piping bag or a zipper top bag with one corner snipped off, fill each tower to the top with whipped cream.*
5. *Level off the top using a small spatula then place towers in the freezer for 1 hour.*
6. *To serve, peel off acetate strips then top with chocolate shavings and serve frozen.*

TIP
If you don't have acetate, use aluminum foil instead and try to keep aluminum foil as smooth as possible.

EASY HAZELNUT SPREAD COOKIES

Makes 24 cookies

Ingredients:

2 cups store-bought hazelnut spread + more for centers

2 large eggs

2 cups all purpose flour

Toasted hazelnuts, for topping

Method:

1. Preheat oven to 350°F and line two sheet pans with parchment paper; set aside.
2. Fit mixer with paddles (no scraper) then add hazelnut spread and eggs.
3. Add outer lid then set timer to 2 minutes.
4. Mix on speed 3 until time is complete.
5. Add flour, reduce to speed 1 then mix for an additional 1 minute.
6. Scoop up 2 tablespoons of dough then place on sheet pan.
7. Repeat with remaining dough then use your thumb to make an indentation into each cookie.
8. Bake for 10-12 minutes or until surface looks dry then remove and let cool.
9. Spoon or pipe additional hazelnut spread into the centers of each cookie, top with hazelnuts and serve.

TIP

To toast hazelnuts, spread out on a sheet pan and bake at 350°F for 15-20 minutes or until lightly browned.

APPLE CAKE

Makes 1 cake

Ingredients:

For the Cake

1 2/3 cups dark brown sugar, packed

2 large eggs

1/2 cup unsweetened applesauce

3/4 cup vegetable oil

2 teaspoons vanilla extract

2 teaspoons baking soda

2 tablespoons apple pie spice

1 1/2 teaspoons kosher salt

1 1/2 pounds Granny Smith apples, skin on, chunked

1 tablespoon fresh lemon juice

1/3 cup dark raisins (optional)

2 1/2 cups all purpose flour

For the Topping

1 cup pecans, chopped

1/4 cup granulated sugar

Method:

1. *Fit mixer with paddles and scraper then add all cake ingredients.*
2. *Add lid then set timer to 5 minutes.*
3. *Mix on speed 3 until time is complete.*
4. *Preheat oven to 350°F and apply nonstick baking spray to a 9x13-inch pan.*
5. *Scrape into pan then top with pecans and granulated sugar.*
6. *Bake for 1 hour or until puffed and internal temperature registers 195°F on a thermometer.*
7. *Remove and serve warm.*

MILLION DOLLAR DIP

Makes 3 1/2 cups

Ingredients:

1 1/2 cups extra sharp Cheddar cheese, shredded

1 1/2 cups mayonnaise

1 cup jarred bacon bits

6 green onions, minced

4 garlic cloves, minced

1/2 cup slivered almonds, toasted

Bottled hot sauce to taste

Kosher salt and fresh pepper to taste

Dippers of your choice

Method:

1. *Fit mixer with paddles and scraper then add all ingredients, except dippers.*
2. *Add lid then set timer to 4 minutes.*
3. *Mix on speed 4 until time is complete.*
4. *Spoon into serving bowl and serve with desired dippers.*

TIP

To toast almonds, spread out on a sheet pan and bake at 350°F for 15-20 minutes or until lightly browned.

SMOKED SALMON DIP ROLL-UPS

Makes 24 roll ups

Ingredients:

2 packages (8 ounces each) cream cheese, softened

1/2 cup unsalted butter, softened

3 ounces smoked salmon, very finely chopped

1 tablespoon chives, minced

Zest and juice of 1 lemon

Kosher salt to taste

2 English cucumbers

Method:

1. *Fit mixer with whisks and scraper then add cream cheese and butter.*
2. *Add outer lid then set timer to 5 minutes.*
3. *Mix on speed 4 for 3 minutes.*
4. *Reduce to speed 3 then add remaining ingredients, except cucumbers, and mix until time is complete.*
5. *Use a vegetable peeler or mandolin to cut strips from cucumbers.*
6. *Spoon a layer of salmon mixture over each cucumber strip.*
7. *Roll up strips in a pinwheel fashion then place on serving plate.*

SAVORY BLUE CHEESE
CHEESECAKE

Makes 1 cake

Ingredients:

1/4 cup bread crumbs

2 packages (8 ounces each) cream cheese, softened

4 ounces blue cheese, softened

1 cup Parmesan cheese, grated

1 bunch green onions, minced

3 garlic cloves, minced

1 tablespoon fresh oregano, minced

Bottled Sriracha hot sauce to taste

2 teaspoons kosher salt

2 teaspoons freshly ground black pepper

4 large eggs

Dippers of your choice

Method:

1. *Preheat oven to 350°F.*
2. *Generously apply nonstick baking spray to the interior of an 8-inch springform pan.*
3. *Scatter bread crumbs over the bottom of the pan; set aside.*
4. *Fit mixer with paddles and scraper then add all the cheeses.*
5. *Add lid then set timer to 6 minutes.*
6. *Mix on speed 4 until time is complete.*
7. *Add remaining ingredients, except dippers, then mix on speed 2 for an additional 2 minutes.*
8. *Pour over bread crumbs then bake for 50 minutes or until just set (cake will jiggle when tapped and will be slightly puffed and beginning to brown). Rotate pan halfway through baking.*
9. *Remove from oven, garnish as desired and serve warm with desired dippers.*

RECIPES

SWEET POTATO
DINNER ROLLS

Makes 24 rolls

Ingredients:

1 cup cold water

1/3 cup bread flour

1 large sweet potato, diced very small

1 cup heavy cream

1/3 cup honey

3 large eggs

3 tablespoons powdered milk

2 tablespoons rapid rise yeast

2 tablespoons kosher salt + more for tops

5 1/2 cups additional bread flour

2 tablespoons unsalted butter, melted + more for tops

Method:

1. *Whisk water and 1/3 cup bread flour together in a small saucepan then turn heat to high.*
2. *Whisk constantly until a full boil is achieved and mixture has thickened.*
3. *Add sweet potato cubes to saucepan, whisk for 30 seconds then remove from heat.*
4. *Fit mixer with dough hook and pusher attachment then add saucepan contents, cream and honey.*
5. *Add outer lid then set timer to 15 minutes.*
6. *Mix on speed 1 for 2 minutes to cool mixture down a bit.*
7. *Add remaining ingredients then mix on speed 3 until time is complete.*
8. *Remove dough hook attachment, cover and let rise for 1 hour.*
9. *Apply nonstick baking spray to two sheet pans; set aside.*
10. *After 1 hour of dough rising, pull dough onto a lightly floured counter.*
11. *Divide dough into 24 pieces, roll into balls then place onto sheet pans.*
12. *Cover and let rise for 30 minutes.*
13. *Preheat oven to 375°F then bake for 18-20 minutes or until well risen and brown.*
14. *Remove, brush rolls with additional melted butter then sprinkle tops with additional salt before serving hot.*

TIP

For plain rolls omit the sweet potato.

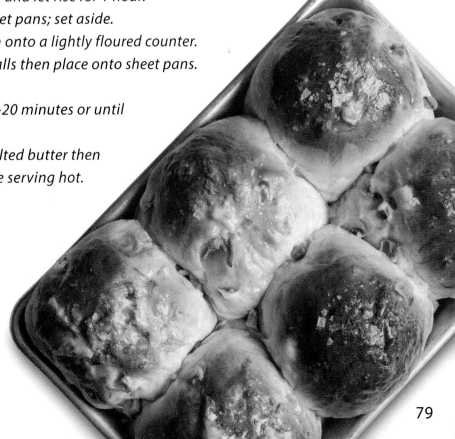

WATERCOLOR
JELLY ROLL CAKE

Makes 1 cake

Ingredients:

For Water Color "Paint"

2 egg whites

1/2 cup cake flour

4 tablespoons unsalted butter, melted

1/2 cup powdered sugar

Food coloring as desired

For the Cake

4 large eggs

3/4 cup granulated sugar

1 teaspoon vanilla extract

3/4 cup all purpose flour

3/4 teaspoon baking powder

1/4 teaspoon kosher salt

Old Fashioned Whipped Cream (see recipe on page 70)

RECIPES

Method:

1. *Apply nonstick baking spray to a 12x17-inch sheet pan and line it with nonstick aluminum foil; set aside.*

2. *In a small bowl whisk together all "paint" ingredients, except food coloring, then color as desired.*

3. *Dot different color "paint" mixture randomly over sheet pan then use a spoon to spread in a thin layer; set aside.*

4. *Preheat oven to 400°F then place an empty sheet pan above the rack you will bake on in order to reflect heat and prevent browning.*

5. *Fit mixer with whisks (no scraper) then add eggs, sugar and vanilla.*

6. *Add outer lid then set timer to 8 minutes.*

7. *Mix on speed 5 until time is complete then remove the whisk attachment.*

8. *Sift flour, baking powder and salt over egg mixture then fold in using a rubber spatula.*

9. *Spread gently and evenly over the "paint" on the sheet pan.*

10. *Bake in center of the oven for 10-12 minutes until cake looks dry on top but is still pale.*

11. *Remove and invert onto plastic wrap then remove aluminum foil.*

12. *Invert again onto a separate piece of plastic wrap then roll up from the short end with both pieces of plastic wrap still in place; let cool.*

13. *Unroll, remove plastic wrap, spread plain side of cake with whipped cream then roll back up to complete the jelly roll.*

14. *Slice and serve as desired.*

CRÈME CAKE WITH GRAPEFRUIT GLAZE

Makes 1 cake

Ingredients:

For the Cake

1 1/2 cups unsalted butter, softened

1 package (8 ounces) cream cheese, softened

3 cups granulated sugar

6 large eggs

2 teaspoons pure vanilla extract

1 teaspoon kosher salt

3 cups unbleached all purpose flour

2 teaspoons baking powder

2 tablespoons matcha powder (optional)

For the Glaze

1 1/2 cups powdered sugar

1 tablespoon Ruby Red grapefruit zest

1 tablespoon Ruby Red grapefruit juice

1 tablespoon Ruby Red grapefruit pulp

A drop of red food coloring (optional)

Method:

1. *Preheat oven to 300°F and generously apply nonstick baking spray to a tube pan; set aside.*
2. *Fit mixer with paddles and scraper then add butter, cream cheese and sugar.*
3. *Add lid then set timer to 8 minutes.*
4. *Mix on speed 3 until time is complete.*
5. *Add eggs then mix on speed 2 for 1 minute.*
6. *Add remaining cake ingredients then mix on speed 1 just until combined.*
7. *Spoon batter into prepared pan.*
8. *Bake for 90 minutes or until brown and a wooden pick inserted in the center emerges clean.*
9. *While cake bakes, stir together all glaze ingredients in a small bowl.*
10. *When baking is complete, remove cake and let cool for 30 minutes.*
11. *Place on a serving plate then spoon glaze over top of cake before serving.*

CHOCOLATE MOUSSE

Makes 6 servings

Ingredients:

2 teaspoons instant coffee

2 cups very cold heavy cream

1/2 cup powdered sugar

1 teaspoon vanilla extract

A pinch of kosher salt

1 cup bittersweet chocolate chips, melted and cooled

Shaved chocolate, raspberries and mint, for serving

Method:

1. *Chill mixer bowl, whisks and scraper for 10 minutes in the refrigerator.*
2. *Fit mixer with whisks and scraper then add coffee, cream, sugar, vanilla and salt.*
3. *Add both pieces of the lid then set timer to 5 minutes (mixing time might be shorter).*
4. *Mix on speed 5 until very soft peaks form.*
5. *While continuing to mix, remove center lid and stream in the cooled but still fluid chocolate quickly.*
6. *As soon as all the chocolate is added, pause mixer then scrape in any unmixed chocolate using a spatula.*
7. *Mix again for 3 seconds without overbeating.*
8. *Spoon into 6 serving cups and chill for a minimum of 1 hour or cover carefully and keep refrigerated for up to 2 days.*
9. *Garnish with shaved chocolate, raspberries and mint before serving.*

SWISS
MERINGUE

Makes about 6 cups meringue

Ingredients:

4 large egg whites

1 cup granulated sugar

Method:

1. *Wash hands, mixer bowl, mixer whisks and anything that will come into contact with the egg whites. Any form of grease, even a small amount of egg yolk will prevent the mixture from getting fluffy and stiff.*

2. *Simmer 1-inch of water in a saucepan over medium heat then rest a stainless steel mixing bowl on the rim of the saucepan to make a double boiler.*

3. *In the double boiler, gently whisk egg whites and sugar together for a few minutes until all grains of sugar have dissolved and mixture is warm (do not let mixture get hot).*

4. *Fit mixer with whisks (no scraper) then add the egg white mixture.*

5. *Add lid then set timer to 8 minutes (mixing time might be shorter).*

6. *Mix on speed 5 until stiff peaks form (tips stand straight up).*

7. *Use meringue within 10 minutes or texture will look curdled.*

CREAM PUFFS

Makes 10 puffs

Ingredients:

1 cup water

1/4 cup unsalted butter

1 teaspoon vanilla extract

1 teaspoon kosher salt

1 tablespoon granulated sugar

1 cup bread flour

4 large eggs

2 large egg whites, divided

Ice cream of your choice

Powdered sugar, for serving

Method:

1. Preheat oven to 425°F and line two sheet pans with parchment paper; set aside.
2. Combine the water, butter, vanilla, salt and sugar in a saucepan and bring to a boil.
3. Using a wooden spoon, stir in all of the flour at once while still over heat then stir vigorously for 1 minute on the stove until a solid dough ball forms; remove from heat then transfer dough to the mixer.
4. Fit mixer with whisks and scraper then add outer lid and set timer to 5 minutes.
5. Mix on speed 4 while adding the eggs, one at a time, then add 1 egg white.
6. When mixture is smooth, pause mixer then test the texture. Pinch up a bit of dough between your thumb and index finger then pull fingers apart to see if dough stretches into a 2-inch strand. If it breaks before 2-inches, add remaining egg white.
7. Spoon 2-inch cream puff dough balls onto prepared sheet pans, 5 balls per pan.
8. Use a wet fork to pat down any points.
9. Bake for 20 minutes, reduce oven temperature to 350°F then bake for an additional 30 minutes or until puffs have tripled in size and are a deep brown color.
10. Remove and let cool then split, fill with ice cream and top with powdered sugar.

FRENCH MACARON COOKIES

Makes about 30 cookie sandwiches

Ingredients:

2 cups powdered sugar

1 cup almond flour

3 large egg whites, at room temperature

1/4 teaspoon cream of tartar

1/8 teaspoon kosher salt

1/4 cup granulated sugar

1 teaspoon vanilla extract

A few drops green food coloring (optional)

Really Easy Buttercream (see recipe on page 18), made with freeze-dried strawberry addition

Method:

1. Line two sheet pans with parchment paper then set aside.
2. Use a fine sifter to sift together the powdered sugar and almond flour.
3. Any pieces of almond flour that do not pass through the sifter should be discarded.
4. Fit clean mixer with clean whisks (no scraper) then add egg whites, cream of tartar and salt.
5. Add outer lid then set timer to 5 minutes (mixing time might be shorter).
6. Mix on speed 5 until foamy.
7. Sprinkle in the granulated sugar and vanilla then continue mixing just until stiff peaks form (tips should stand straight up).
8. Remove bowl and whisks from mixer then gently fold in almond flour mixture and food coloring using a rubber spatula until thoroughly mixed together (mixture is right when a spoonful of batter dropped onto batter in the bowl takes approximately 10 seconds to fully smooth out).
9. Scrape mixture into a pastry bag fitted with a round 1/2-inch tip then pipe out sixty 1-inch cookies about 1-inch apart.
10. Let stand at room temperature until the tops of the cookies are dry to the touch (about 1 hour depending on your humidity levels).
11. Preheat oven to 275°F then bake cookies, one sheet pan at a time, for 18-22 minutes or until dry to the touch (they should not color).
12. Remove and let cool completely before sandwiching with buttercream.
13. Serve the day they are made.

REAL FRENCH ONION
DIP

Makes 2 1/2 cups

Ingredients:

3 tablespoons unsalted butter

3 large yellow onions, sliced

Kosher salt and fresh pepper to taste

1 1/2 cups sour cream

1 teaspoon Worcestershire sauce

1 bunch fresh chives, minced

Assorted chips, for serving

Method:

1. *Place butter and onions into a large skillet over medium heat.*
2. *Sauté for 25 minutes stirring frequently or until darkly caramelized.*
3. *Remove from heat then let cool for 10 minutes.*
4. *Fit mixer with whisks and scraper then add all ingredients, except chips, to the mixer.*
5. *Add lid then set timer to 2 minutes.*
6. *Mix on speed 3 until time is complete.*
7. *Garnish as desired and serve with chips.*

TIP

Avoid using Vidalia or other very sweet onions or the dip will turn out sweet instead of savory.

WHIPPED CORN & RICOTTA
DIP

Makes 3 1/2 cups

Ingredients:

1 1/2 cups fresh corn kernels

1 1/2 cups whole milk ricotta cheese

1 tablespoon honey

2 tablespoons fresh lemon juice

2 tablespoons white miso paste (optional)

2 green onions, chopped

1 garlic clove, minced

Bottled hot sauce to taste

Kosher salt and fresh pepper to taste

1/4 teaspoon fresh thyme, chopped

Dippers of your choice

Method:

1. *Fit mixer with whisks and scraper then add all ingredients, except dippers.*
2. *Add lid then set timer to 4 minutes.*
3. *Mix on speed 5 until time is complete.*
4. *Spoon into serving bowl then serve with desired dippers.*

BACON HORSERADISH
DIP

Makes 3 cups

Ingredients:

1 package (8 ounces) cream cheese, softened

1/2 cup sour cream

1/2 cup mayonnaise

3 tablespoons bacon grease (optional)

1/3 cup prepared horseradish

Kosher salt and fresh pepper to taste

1 tablespoon fresh lemon juice

1 teaspoon Worcestershire sauce

1 bunch green onions, chopped

10 bacon slices, cooked and crumbled

Dippers of your choice

Method:

1. *Fit mixer with whisks and scraper then add all ingredients, except dippers.*
2. *Add lid then set timer to 2 minutes.*
3. *Mix on speed 4 until time is complete.*
4. *Scrape mixture into a serving bowl.*
5. *Garnish as desired and serve with desired dippers.*

CHEDDAR BISCUITS

Makes 16 biscuits

Ingredients:

3 cups all purpose flour

1 tablespoon granulated sugar

1 tablespoon + 1 teaspoon baking powder

2 teaspoons kosher salt + more for tops

1 teaspoon freshly ground pepper

2 1/2 cups heavy cream + more for tops

2 tablespoons fresh oregano

1 bunch green onions, chopped

1/2 cup fresh parsley, chopped

1/2 cup Parmesan cheese, shredded

2 cups sharp Cheddar cheese, shredded

Method:

1. Preheat oven to 375°F and line two sheet pans with parchment paper; set aside.
2. Fit mixer with paddles and scraper then add all ingredients.
3. Add lid then set timer to 3 minutes.
4. Mix on speed 3 until time is complete.
5. On a piece of plastic wrap, pat out dough into a 1-inch thick rectangle.
6. Cut dough into 1 1/2-inch squares then place on the prepared sheet pans.
7. Brush additional cream on top of each biscuit then sprinkle with additional salt.
8. Bake for 15-20 minutes or until well browned and puffed.
9. Remove and serve hot.

BEST
SHEPHERD'S PIE

Makes 4-6 servings

Ingredients:

1 tablespoon olive oil

1 large yellow onion, chopped

1 pound ground beef

Kosher salt and fresh pepper to taste

1/2 teaspoon dried sage

2 tablespoons all purpose flour or cornstarch

1 1/2 cups beef stock

1 tablespoon soy sauce

2 tablespoons ketchup

1 bag (12 ounces) frozen mixed vegetables, thawed

Mashed Potatoes (see recipe on page 12)

Method:

1. *Place oil, onions and beef into a large skillet over medium-high heat.*
2. *Stir to break up beef and cook until no pink color remains.*
3. *Add salt, pepper, sage and flour then stir until no flour is visible.*
4. *Add beef stock, soy sauce and ketchup then stir until thick and bubbly.*
5. *Stir in mixed vegetables then transfer mixture into an oven-safe casserole dish; set aside.*
6. *Preheat oven to 400°F.*
7. *Pipe or spoon mashed potatoes on top of beef mixture in the casserole dish.*
8. *Bake for 20 minutes or until brown and bubbly.*
9. *Remove, garnish as desired and serve hot.*

KITCHEN SINK COOKIES

Makes 4 dozen cookies

Ingredients:

1 cup unsalted butter, softened

1 cup dark brown sugar, packed

3/4 cup granulated sugar

2 large eggs

1 teaspoon vanilla extract

1/2 teaspoon kosher salt

1 teaspoon baking soda

1 teaspoon baking powder

1 2/3 cups all purpose flour

1 cup dark raisins

1 cup chocolate chips

1 cup chocolate candies

1 cup old fashioned rolled oats

1 cup pecan pieces, toasted

Method:

1. *Preheat oven to 375°F and line two sheet pans with parchment paper; set aside.*
2. *Fit mixer with paddles and scraper then add butter, both sugars, eggs and vanilla.*
3. *Add lid then set timer to 6 minutes.*
4. *Mix on speed 3 for 4 minutes then reduce to speed 1 and add remaining ingredients.*
5. *Mix just until combined then use an ice cream scoop to make golf ball size cookies and place on prepared sheet pans 2-inches apart.*
6. *Bake for 12-15 minutes or until puffed and light golden brown.*
7. *Remove and let cool until warm before serving.*

TIP

To toast pecans, spread out on a sheet pan and bake at 350°F for 15-20 minutes or until lightly browned.

SPRINKLE
MARSHMALLOWS

Makes about 40 marshmallows

Ingredients:

Cornstarch for pan and tops

2 tablespoons + 1 teaspoon plain, unflavored gelatin

3 tablespoons cold water

1 2/3 cups granulated sugar

2/3 cup additional cold water

1 1/2 cups light corn syrup

3 large egg whites

2 teaspoons butter vanilla extract

Sprinkles, for rolling

Method:

1. *Sift an even, heavy layer of cornstarch over a 1/4 sheet pan; set aside.*
2. *In a small bowl, quickly whisk together gelatin and 3 tablespoons water; let stand for 5 minutes.*
3. *Fit mixer with whisks (no scraper) then break up the now solid gelatin and add to the mixer.*
4. *Add outer lid, set timer to 15 minutes but do not start mixing.*
5. *In a large saucepan, combine sugar, remaining 2/3 cup water and corn syrup.*
6. *Place over high heat and stir briefly to moisten all the sugar.*
7. *Boil without stirring to 240°F or just above the soft-ball stage (about 6-8 minutes).*
8. *Remove from heat then immediately, but carefully, pour hot syrup over gelatin in the mixer.*
9. *Start mixer on speed 1 then gradually increase to speed 5.*
10. *Add egg whites and vanilla then continue to mix until volume quadruples and mixture is shiny but still fluid.*
11. *Remove and scrape marshmallow onto cornstarch-lined pan without disturbing cornstarch.*
12. *Sift a layer of cornstarch over top then set aside for 2 hours to cool and firm up.*
13. *Sift a layer of cornstarch over a large cutting board.*
14. *Using your fingers, pull the sheet of marshmallows from the pan onto the cutting board.*
15. *Sift more cornstarch over the top then use a large chef's knife to cut marshmallow into squares.*
16. *Roll each square in sprinkles.*
17. *Store marshmallows in an airtight container at room temperature for up to 1 week.*

TIP

If you are trying to avoid dyes that are commonly found in colored sprinkles, you can find great tasting all-natural sprinkles at health food stores or online.

VANILLA
TALL CAKE

Makes 1 cake

Ingredients:

1 3/4 cups granulated sugar

1 cup unsalted butter, softened

1 teaspoon kosher salt

1 tablespoon baking powder

1 teaspoon vanilla extract

1/4 teaspoon butter extract

5 large egg whites

2 3/4 cups cake flour

1 cup whole milk

Really Easy Buttercream (see recipe on page 18)

Food coloring as desired

Method:

1. *Preheat oven to 350°F then apply nonstick baking spray to three 6-inch round cake pans; set aside.*

2. *Fit mixer with whisks and scraper then add sugar, butter, salt and baking powder.*

3. *Add lid then set timer to 7 minutes.*

4. *Mix on speed 3 for 5 minutes.*

5. *Add the extracts and egg whites then mix on speed 3 for 1 minute.*

6. *Add remaining ingredients, except buttercream and food coloring, while mixing on speed 1 until just blended (about 1 minute).*

7. *Divide batter evenly between pans.*

8. *Bake for 20-25 minutes or until a wooden pick inserted off-center comes out with just a few moist crumbs clinging to it.*

9. *Remove and let cool for 10 minutes before removing from pans then let cool completely.*

10. *Fill, stack and frost cake layers then use a small off-set spatula to apply random patches of colored buttercream around bottom third of cake. Use a spatula to pull swaths of buttercream upwards.*

CHEESEBURGER PINWHEELS

Makes 8 servings

Ingredients:

1 tablespoon unsalted butter

1 pound ground beef

1 large yellow onion, chopped

3 cups all purpose flour

1 tablespoon granulated sugar

1 tablespoon + 1 teaspoon baking powder

2 teaspoons kosher salt

1 teaspoon freshly ground pepper

2 1/2 cups heavy cream

1/3 cup ketchup

2 tablespoons yellow mustard

2 tablespoons dill pickle relish

2 cups sharp Cheddar cheese, shredded

Method:

1. In a large skillet over medium-high heat, add butter, beef and onions.
2. Stir to break up beef then cook until no pink color remains; drain and let cool.
3. Preheat oven to 375°F and line two sheet pans with parchment paper; set aside.
4. Fit mixer with paddles and scraper then add flour, sugar, baking powder, salt, pepper and cream.
5. Add lid then set timer to 3 minutes.
6. Mix on speed 3 until time is complete.
7. On a piece of plastic wrap, pat out dough into a 14x9-inch rectangle.
8. Top with ketchup, mustard, pickle relish and cheese.
9. Top with beef mixture then roll up in a jelly roll fashion.
10. Cut dough into 8 pinwheels then place on the prepared sheet pans.
11. Bake for 20-25 minutes or until well browned and puffed.
12. Remove and serve hot.

PIMENTO
CHEESE DIP

Makes 3 1/2 cups

Ingredients:

1 jar (4 ounces) diced pimientos, drained

1 package (8 ounces) cream cheese, softened

1/2 cup mayonnaise

1 tablespoon fresh lemon juice

1 tablespoon ketchup

2 cups extra-sharp Cheddar cheese, shredded

2 tablespoons yellow onions, minced

Hot sauce to taste

Kosher salt and fresh pepper to taste

Method:

1. *Fit mixer with paddles and scraper then add all ingredients.*
2. *Add lid and set timer to 4 minutes.*
3. *Mix on speed 3 until time is complete.*
4. *Use as a dip or spread if desired.*

SEEDED
RAISIN BREAD

Makes 1 large loaf

Ingredients:

2/3 cups whole milk

1 tablespoon rapid rise yeast

1/4 cup powdered milk

1/4 cup molasses

1/2 teaspoon apple cider vinegar

2 tablespoons cocoa powder

1 large egg

1 1/2 tablespoons unsalted butter, melted

1 1/2 cups bread flour

1 cup whole wheat flour

1/4 cup dark raisins

1/4 cup dried apricots, chopped

1/4 cup walnuts

Method:

1. *Apply nonstick baking spray to a loaf pan.*
2. *Fit mixer with dough hook and pusher attachment then add all ingredients.*
3. *Add lid then set timer to 12 minutes.*
4. *Mix on speed 1 until time is complete.*
5. *Remove dough hook attachment, cover and let rise for 40 minutes.*
6. *Place dough in loaf pan, cover and let rise again for 40 minutes.*
7. *Preheat oven to 350°F then bake in the lower third of the oven for 1 hour or until well risen and internal temperature registers 200°F on a thermometer.*
8. *Remove and let cool before serving.*

CHEESY
PRETZEL BITES

Makes 24 bites

Ingredients:

For the Dough

1 cup beer

2 tablespoons olive oil

1 tablespoon rapid rise yeast

1/4 cup powdered milk

1/4 teaspoon apple cider vinegar

1 tablespoon kosher salt

1 tablespoon dark brown sugar

1 large egg

3 cups unbleached bread flour

For the Filling and Brushing

6 sticks string cheese, cut each into 4 pieces

1 teaspoon granulated garlic

2 tablespoons baking soda

1 cup hot water

Coarse salt, for sprinkling

Method:

1. *Fit mixer with the dough hook and pusher attachment then add all dough ingredients.*
2. *Add lid then set timer to 10 minutes.*
3. *Mix on speed 2 until time is complete.*
4. *Remove dough hook attachment, cover and let rise for 1 hour or until doubled in bulk.*
5. *Line a sheet pan with parchment paper; set aside.*
6. *Remove dough, roll into a large 1 1/2 to 2-inch thick rope then cut into 24 pieces.*
7. *Press a piece of string cheese in the center of each dough ball then add a pinch of garlic.*
8. *Pinch to seal cheese inside dough ball then place seam-side down on sheet pan; repeat with remaining dough.*
9. *In a small bowl stir together the baking soda and hot water.*
10. *Brush a bit of this mixture on the tops of each dough ball then sprinkle with coarse salt.*
11. *Cover and let rise for 30 minutes.*
12. *Preheat oven to 400°F then bake in lower third of oven for 15-20 minutes or until puffed and well-browned.*
13. *Remove and serve warm.*

CHERRY UPSIDE DOWN CAKE

Makes 8 servings

Ingredients:

1 3/4 cups granulated sugar

1/2 cup unsalted butter, softened + more for pan

1/2 cup solid white shortening

1 teaspoon kosher salt

1 tablespoon baking powder

1 teaspoon vanilla extract

1/4 teaspoon butter extract

1/8 teaspoon almond extract

5 large egg whites

2 3/4 cups cake flour

1 cup whole milk

1/2 cup clear corn syrup

3 cups jarred maraschino cherries, well drained

Method:

1. *Preheat oven to 350°F and generously apply nonstick baking spray to the inside of a 12-inch skillet or cake pan; set aside.*
2. *Fit mixer with paddles and scraper then add sugar, butter, shortening, salt and baking powder.*
3. *Add outer lid then set timer to 8 minutes.*
4. *Mix on speed 3 for 5 minutes, pause then add extracts and eggs then mix until smooth.*
5. *Pause again, add flour and milk then mix on speed 2 until just blended.*
6. *Pour 4 tablespoons melted butter into the bottom of the skillet or cake pan.*
7. *Refrigerate until butter has hardened then pour corn syrup over butter.*
8. *Pour cherries over the corn syrup and work into an even, tightly packed layer.*
9. *Spoon batter into cherry-covered skillet or pan until all cherries are covered.*
10. *Place a rack in the upper portion of the oven then place an empty sheet pan on this rack (this will shield the cake from overbrowning).*
11. *Bake cake in the lower third of the oven for 60-70 minutes or until browned and a wooden pick inserted off-center comes out with just a few moist crumbs clinging to it.*
12. *Remove and cool for 30 minutes.*
13. *Carefully invert cake onto a rimmed serving plate and serve as desired.*

TIP

You can bake this cake in a variety of vessels. For the on-air TV presentations, I typically bake this cake in a Wolfgang Puck skillet or omelet pan as the curved shape makes for a particularly beautiful cake.

BANANA CREAM PIE

Makes one 8-inch pie

Ingredients:

3 cups half & half, cold

2 boxes (4 ounces each) instant banana pudding mix

4 ripe bananas, sliced

A store-bought graham cracker crust

2 cups heavy whipping cream, cold

1/3 cup granulated sugar

2 teaspoons pure vanilla extract

Method:

1. *Fit mixer with whisks and scraper then add half & half and pudding mix.*
2. *Add lid then set timer to 2 minutes.*
3. *Mix on speed 4 until time is complete then fold in bananas using a spatula.*
4. *Scrape mixture into crust then smooth the top.*
5. *Wash the mixer bowl, whisks and scraper then reassemble and add remaining ingredients.*
6. *Add lid then set timer to 3 minutes (mixing time might be shorter).*
7. *Mix on speed 5 until semi-stiff peaks form (test by stopping mixer and pulling mixture up using a spoon).*
8. *Pipe or spread whipped cream over banana mixture then serve within 1 hour before bananas begin to darken.*

PIÑA COLADA FRUIT DIP

Makes 3 cups

Ingredients:

2 packages (8 ounces each) cream cheese, softened

1 jar (7 ounces) marshmallow crème

1 cup fresh pineapple, chopped

1/2 cup coconut flakes

Dippers of your choice

Method:

1. *Fit mixer with whisks (no scraper) then add cream cheese and marshmallow crème.*
2. *Add outer lid then set timer to 5 minutes.*
3. *Mix on speed 4 for 4 minutes.*
4. *Reduce to speed 3 then add remaining ingredients, except dippers, and mix until time is complete.*
5. *Spoon into a serving bowl.*
6. *Serve with desired dippers.*

TIP

To make it look as pictured, save pineapple shell and use as a serving vessel.

NO BAKE RASPBERRY SWIRL CHEESECAKE

Makes 8 servings

Ingredients:

1/4 cup vanilla cookie crumbs

4 packages (8 ounces each) cream cheese, softened

1 1/2 cups powdered sugar

1 tablespoon fresh lemon juice

2 packets (1/2-ounce each) unflavored gelatin

1/2 cup heavy cream

1 cup frozen raspberries, thawed

1/2 cup granulated sugar

Method:

1. Apply nonstick cooking spray to a 7-inch springform pan then scatter cookie crumbs into the pan; set aside.
2. Fit mixer with whisks and scraper then add cream cheese, powdered sugar and lemon juice.
3. Add lid then set timer to 10 minutes.
4. Mix on speed 3 for 8 minutes.
5. Whisk together the gelatin and cream in a microwave-safe bowl and let stand for 5 minutes.
6. Microwave for 1-2 minutes or until no grains of gelatin remain.
7. Mix on speed 3 for remaining 2 minutes while streaming the gelatin mixture into the cream cheese mixture until smooth.
8. In a separate bowl, stir together the raspberries and granulated sugar.
9. Layer cream cheese mixture and raspberry mixture into the prepared springform pan.
10. Freeze for a minimum of 2 hours before serving.

CRISPY SWEET
CORN FRITTERS

Makes 4 servings

Ingredients:

3 large egg whites

1/4 teaspoon cream of tartar

1/4 cup granulated sugar

3 large eggs yolks

2 tablespoons unsalted butter, melted

2 cups corn kernels

1 teaspoon vanilla extract

1/2 cup buttermilk

1 1/2 cups all purpose flour

1 1/2 teaspoons kosher salt

2 teaspoons baking powder

Vegetable oil, for frying

Powdered sugar, for serving

Method:

1. *Fit clean mixer with clean whisks (no scraper) then add egg whites.*
2. *Add outer lid then set timer to 5 minutes (mixing time might be shorter).*
3. *Mix on speed 3 until foamy then add cream of tartar and sugar.*
4. *Mix until stiff peaks form then set aside.*
5. *In a separate mixing bowl, whisk together remaining ingredients, except vegetable oil and powdered sugar.*
6. *Fold in the egg whites using a rubber spatula just until uniform in color.*
7. *Preheat vegetable oil in fryer to 350°F following manufacturer's directions.*
8. *Drop batter by the spoonful into oil.*
9. *Fry a few fritters at a time for 2-4 minutes until golden brown, turning them over halfway through frying.*
10. *Remove and let drain on a wire rack set over absorbent paper on a sheet pan.*
11. *Repeat with remaining batter then top with powdered sugar and serve hot.*

ZUCCHINI MUFFINS

Makes 12 muffins

Ingredients:

1/2 cup vegetable oil

1 cup granulated sugar

2 large eggs

1 teaspoon vanilla extract

3 tablespoons sour cream

2 cups zucchini, grated and drained

1/2 cup toasted walnuts, chopped (optional)

2 cups unbleached all purpose flour

1/2 teaspoon ground cinnamon

1 teaspoon baking soda

1/2 teaspoon baking powder

1/2 teaspoon kosher salt

Method:

1. Preheat oven to 350°F and line a muffin pan with cupcake liners.
2. Fit mixer with whisks and scraper then add the oil, sugar and eggs.
3. Add outer lid then set timer to 6 minutes.
4. Mix on speed 4 for 4 minutes.
5. Add vanilla, sour cream and zucchini then mix on speed 2 just until incorporated.
6. Reduce to speed 1 then add remaining ingredients and mix just until no flour remains visible.
7. Fill each cupcake liner 3/4 full of batter.
8. Bake for 20-25 minutes or until browned and a wooden pick inserted in the center emerges clean.
9. Remove and serve warm.

SOURCE PAGE

Here are some of my favorite places to find ingredients that are not readily available at grocery stores as well as kitchen tools and supplies that help you become a better cook.

The Bakers Catalogue at King Arthur Flour

Gel or paste food colorings, pastry bags, baking pans, cake pans, silicone spring loaded cookie cutters, blowtorches, rubber and silicone spatulas, digital timers, meringue powder, oven thermometers, candy thermometers, the best instant read thermometers, off-set spatulas, measuring cups and spoons, knives, cookie sheets, jimmies and sprinkles
www.kingarthurflour.com

Wilton Enterprises

Everything needed for cake decorating. Cake decorating turntables, cake pans, spatulas, cake icer tips, colored sugars, sprinkles, gel and paste food coloring, edible gold luster dust, sprinkles, fondant, gum paste, royal icing mix, meringue powder, cake scrapers and side smoothers, decorating tips, piping bags and couplers. Wilton also sells many of their supplies at Michael's crafts, Jo-Ann crafts and Walmart.
www.wilton.com

Vanilla From Tahiti

My favorite pure vanilla extract and the best quality vanilla beans
www.vanillafromtahiti.com

Whole Foods

Natural food coloring, natural sprinkles, natural and organic baking ingredients, natural parchment paper, good quality chocolate such as Valhrona and Callebaut
www.wholefoods.com

Kerekes the Chef Station

All varieties of cake pans, edible gold luster dust, spatulas, cake decorating turntables, cake scrapers and cake side smoothers
www.bakedeco.com

Chocosphere

Excellent quality cocoa (Callebaut), all Chocolates, Jimmies and sprinkles
www.chocosphere.com

A

Alaska, Easy Baked 13
Animal Crackers, Old Fashioned 68
Animal Cupcakes 26
Apple Cake 75
Artichoke Dip, Spinach 47

B

Bacon Horseradish Dip 90
Bacon Wrapped Meatloaf 20
Baked Alaska, Easy 13
Ball, Cheese 14
Ball, Halloween Cheese 22
Banana Cream Pie 104
Basic White Bread 40
BBQ Chicken Cheesy Bread 61
Best Shepherd's Pie 92
Biscuits, Cheddar 91
Bites, Cheesy Pretzel 101
Blue Cheese Cheesecake, Savory 78
Boats, Buffalo Chicken Mini 45
Bread, BBQ Chicken Cheesy 61
Bread, Carrot Raisin 62
Bread, Cheddar Bacon Jalapeño 32
Bread, Multigrain 35
Bread, Seeded Raisin 100
Brioche, Oliver's Gluten-Free 48
Broiled Oatmeal Cake 58
Brownies, Mocha Fudge 57
Buffalo Chicken Mini Boats 45
Bullseye Cheesecake 28
Buttercream, Really Easy 18

C

Cactus Cupcakes, Chocolate 56
Cake, Apple 75
Cake, Broiled Oatmeal 58
Cake, Cherry Upside Down 102
Cake, Chocolate Rainbow 19
Cake, Crème Cake with Grapefruit 82
Cake, Lava 42
Cake, Lemon Pound 37
Cake, Mixing Bowl Rose 10
Cake, Old Fashioned Blueberry Coffee 52
Cake, Vanilla Tall 96
Cake, Watercolor Jelly Roll 80
Carrot Raisin Bread 62
Cheddar Bacon Jalapeño Bread 32
Cheddar Biscuits 91
Cheese Ball 14
Cheese Ball, Halloween 22
Cheeseburger Pinwheels 98
Cheesecake, Bullseye 28
Cheesecake, No Bake Raspberry Swirl 106
Cheesecake, Savory Blue Cheese 78
Cheese Dip, Pimento 99
Cheese Soufflé 38
Cheesy Pretzel Bites 101
Cherry Ice Cream, No Churn 50
Cherry Upside Down Cake 102
Chicken Cheesy Bread, BBQ 61
Chocolate Cactus Cupcakes 56
Chocolate Chip Cookies, Oatmeal 34
Chocolate Meringue Pie 16

Chocolate Mousse 83
Chocolate Rainbow Cake 19
Chocolate Towers, Triple Layered 73
Cinnamon Rolls 67
Cobbler, Easy Fruit 36
Coffee Cake, Old Fashioned Blueberry 52
Cookies, Crinkle 53
Cookies, Easy Hazelnut Spread 74
Cookies, French Macaron 86
Cookies, Iced Sugar 24
Cookies, Kitchen Sink 93
Cookies, Oatmeal Chocolate Chip 34
Cookies, Peanut Butter & Jelly 31
Cookies, Wolfgang's Favorite 49
Cornbread, Jalapeño 44
Corn Fritters, Crispy Sweet 107
Corn & Ricotta Dip, Whipped 89
Crackers, Old Fashioned Animal 68
Cream Pie, Banana 104
Cream Puffs 85
Crème Cake with Grapefruit Glaze 82
Crinkle Cookies 53
Crispy Sweet Corn Fritters 107
Cupcakes, Animal 26
Cupcakes, Chocolate Cactus 56
Cupcakes, Melted Snowman 54

D

Date Oat Energy Bites 41
Dessert "Lasagna", Strawberry 30
Dinner Rolls, Sweet Potato 79
Dip, Bacon Horseradish 90
Dip, Million Dollar 76
Dip, Pimento Cheese 99
Dip, Piña Colada Fruit 105
Dip, Real French Onion 88
Dip, Spinach Artichoke 47
Dip, Whipped Corn & Ricotta 89
Dough, Pizza 65
Dulce de Leche Pie 66

E

Easy Baked Alaska 13
Easy Fruit Cobbler 36
Easy Hazelnut Spread Cookies 74
Energy Bites, Date Oat 41

F

Focaccia, Meatloaf 64
Freezer Pie, Limeade 72
French Macaron Cookies 86
French Onion Dip, Real 88
Fritters, Crispy Sweet Corn 107
Fruit Cobbler, Easy 36
Fruit Dip, Piña Colada 105
Fudge Brownies, Mocha 57

G

Gluten-Free Brioche, Oliver's 48
Grandma's Meatballs 60
Grapefruit Glaze, Crème Cake with 82

H

Halloween Cheese Ball 22

INDEX

Hazelnut Spread Cookies, Easy 74
Homemade Pie Crust 71
Horseradish Dip, Bacon 90

I

Ice Cream, No Churn Cherry 50
Iced Sugar Cookies 24

J

Jalapeño Bread, Cheddar Bacon 32
Jalapeño Cornbread 44
Jelly Roll Cake, Watercolor 80

K

Kitchen Sink Cookies 93
Kugelhopf, Wolfgang's 21

L

"Lasagna", Strawberry Dessert 30
Lava Cake 42
Lemon Pound Cake 37
Limeade Freezer Pie 72
Limoncello & Raspberry Semifreddo 17

M

Macaron Cookies, French 86
Marshmallows, Sprinkle 94
Mashed Potatoes 12
Mashed Potato "Frosted" Meatloaf 63
Meatballs, Grandma's 60
Meatloaf, Bacon Wrapped 20
Meatloaf, Mashed Potato "Frosted" 63
Melted Snowman Cupcakes 54
Meringue Pie, Chocolate 16
Meringue, Swiss 84
Million Dollar Dip 76
Mini Boats, Buffalo Chicken 45
Mixing Bowl Rose Cake 10
Mocha Fudge Brownies 57
Mousse, Chocolate 83
Muffins, Zucchini 108
Multigrain Bread 35

N

No Bake Raspberry Swirl Cheesecake 106
No Churn Cherry Ice Cream 50

O

Oat Energy Bites, Date 41
Oatmeal Cake, Broiled 58
Oatmeal Chocolate Chip Cookies 34
Old Fashioned Animal Crackers 68
Old Fashioned Blueberry Coffee Cake 52
Old Fashioned Whipped Cream 70
Oliver's Gluten-Free Brioche 48

P

Parfait, Pumpkin Mousse 27
Peanut Butter & Jelly Cookies 31
Pecan Mashed Sweet Potatoes 46
Pie, Banana Cream 104
Pie, Chocolate Meringue 16
Pie Crust, Homemade 71

Pie, Dulce de Leche 66
Pie, Limeade Freezer 72
Pimento Cheese Dip 99
Piña Colada Fruit Dip 105
Pinwheels, Cheeseburger 98
Pizza Dough 65
Potatoes, Mashed 12
Potatoes, Pecan Mashed Sweet 46
Pretzel Bites, Cheesy 101
Puffs, Cream 85
Pumpkin Mousse Parfait 27

R

Rainbow Cake, Chocolate 19
Raisin Bread, Carrot 62
Raisin Bread, Seeded 100
Raspberry Swirl Cheesecake, No Bake 106
Real French Onion Dip 88
Really Easy Buttercream 18
Rolls, Cinnamon 67
Rolls, Sweet Potato Dinner 79
Roll-Ups, Smoked Salmon Dip 77
Rose Cake, Mixing Bowl 10

S

Salmon Dip Roll-Ups, Smoked 77
Savory Blue Cheese Cheesecake 78
Seeded Raisin Bread 100
Semifreddo, Limoncello & Raspberry 17
Shepherd's Pie, Best 92
Smoked Salmon Dip Roll-Ups 77
Snowman Cupcakes, Melted 54
Soufflé, Cheese 38
Spinach Artichoke Dip 47
Sprinkle Marshmallows 94
Strawberry Dessert "Lasagna" 30
Sugar Cookies, Iced 24
Sweet Potato Dinner Rolls 79
Sweet Potatoes, Pecan Mashed 46
Swiss Meringue 84

T

Tall Cake, Vanilla 96
Tomato Focaccia 64
Towers, Triple Layered Chocolate 73
Triple Layered Chocolate Towers 73

U

Upside Down Cake, Cherry 102

V

Vanilla Tall Cake 96

W

Watercolor Jelly Roll Cake 80
Whipped Corn & Ricotta Dip 89
Whipped Cream, Old Fashioned 70
White Bread, Basic 40
Wolfgang's Favorite Cookies 49
Wolfgang's Kugelhopf 21

Z

Zucchini Muffins 108

INDEX

FOR ALL OF MARIAN GETZ'S
COOKBOOKS AS WELL AS
COOKWARE, APPLIANCES, CUTLERY
AND KITCHEN ACCESSORIES
BY WOLFGANG PUCK

PLEASE VISIT
HSN.COM
(KEYWORD: WOLFGANG PUCK)